A SMILE HERE, A TEAR THERE

John J. McCullagh

A smile here, a tear there

the columba press

First published in 1998 by
the columba press
55a Spruce Avenue, Stillorgan Industrial Park,
Blackrock, Co Dublin

Cover by Bill Bolger
Illustrations by Kieran McGlynn
Origination by The Columba Press
Printed in Ireland by Colour Books Ltd, Dublin

ISBN 1 85607 244 4

Contents

15 August 1998
Dedicated
to
those who lost their lives,
those who lost their loved ones,
and all who will carry the scars
of Omagh
for life

Opportunities disguised

The old sycamore in the grounds of our two-roomed primary school, in the mountains of County Tyrone, was there by an act of God, the teacher would tell us. The occasional motorist or horse cart passing the school could not distract us. That all changed when endless convoys of American troops made their way to camp on the mountains before setting off for war in Europe in the early forties. This passage from the gospel of Luke gave me an idea. I put all the faith a young boy could muster into removing the tree for a better view – but it never strained a root. Either my faith was weak or the Atlantic ocean was too far to the west.

> He said to his disciples if your brother does something wrong, reprove him, and if he is sorry, forgive him. And if he wrongs you seven times a day and seven times comes back to you and says, 'I am sorry,' you must forgive him. The apostles said to the Lord, 'Increase our faith.' The Lord replied, 'Were your faith the size of a mustard seed, you could say to this mulberry tree, be uprooted and planted in the sea, and it would obey you.'
> Lk 17:1-6.

I never tested my faith on Mullacharn or Sawel mountain, as I was happy with their beauty and majestic protection. In Ireland we tend to colour events and the language is rich in exaggeration. We have that in common with the eastern countries, where language is no less vivid. Jesus Christ did not envisage mountains and mulberry bushes in a constant state of transit. His simple point was that the impossible becomes possible if approached with faith. Through faith, the power of God is at our disposal. Mao Tse-tung told the people of China that Christians had prayed for the removal of mountains but the mountains stayed their ground, but 'we,' he said, 'we moved the mountains with our own hands.' Perhaps he had in mind the Chinese proverb, 'The man who moved the mountain began by carrying away small stones.'

Across the country for too many years, many mountains have cast their shadows over all of us – mountains of uncertainty, forbidding peaks of family friction and neighbourhood tensions, the threatening pinnacles of violence and community division. It would be nonsensical naïvete on the part of a Christian if he or she felt that these problems could have been prayed away without any other contribution to the community and the country.

I saw a mountain of hate begin to crumble in Northern Ireland because a group of young people decided to cross useless dividing lines, when they discovered that their praise of God was pointless if they remained singing hymns in harmony while the chants of hate rang out obscene messages of division. With faith in their God and a growing faith in each other, they began to carry the small stones. Maybe the cynic who lives in the age of the giant earthmoving plant will smile at the effort – but the giants of state across the world have either moved little or have added to the mountain range that goes on dividing people.

'Without me,' says Christ, 'you can do nothing.' With him, all things are possible and whatever hilltop blacks out the sun of joy from our lives, it is vulnerable to men and women who, with faith, will demolish it with bare hands. These mountains, in the words of one American writer, are great opportunities brilliantly disguised as impossible situations. These were the sentiments of Jeremiah the prophet whose testament we make our prayer for any day.

> Ah Sovereign Lord, you have made the heavens and the earth
> By your great power and outstretched arm.
> Nothing is too difficult for you –
> Not even our mountains. Amen.

Saint ...?

All Saints Day brings her back to mind, for I know that I can now say I knew a saint once. She grew up in the years before the war and poverty was a boarder with them in the remote farm where the family scraped a thin living from the ungenerous land. When her mother and father died from tuberculosis, she left home to work in the city, worn out with two years of nursing them in the white-washed outhouse, and still haunted by the terrible loneliness when her sister and brothers took the emigrant boat to America in 1946. The evening of her marriage, she went past her old home on the way to a honeymoon of two days in Bundoran, and found that the thatch roof had caved in and the fireplace was silent. The white-washed outhouse had fallen down.

Her marriage was punctuated by pain. She had to work through the three pregnancies up to a fortnight before the births and, wane and tired, she came back to the factory so that her children could have some of the luxuries in life she was denied. The emigrant planes stole the three children in time and she nursed her husband, left brittle by a stroke, until he died on a bleak winter morning.

Now, on her own, with the occasional family greeting from Australia and America, she watched violence spread through her country like the malignant cancer that it was. In her own words, she took to prayer, and the names of the victims and their families were enfolded in her daily cry to God which went on for hour after hour every day. Her last prayer at night was for those who planned death and division. She wrote the names into her book of prayer, the names culled from the morning papers, but she had to give that up when a hundred died. If the tragedy was local she would send her pension money anonymously and would fast on the funeral day.

Throughout all this, she remained a neighbour of great good humour and was a source of rich wisdom to the young folk who called with her. 'When the peace comes we will have to pray twice as much for forgiveness,' she told me over and over again, and she wrote into the little space left in her book a quotation I gave her from the great English saint and statesman, Thomas More:

The good which people do to us we write in sand –
the harm they do we carve in marble.

'We'll pray,' she said often, 'that the carved stones will be overgrown in time with understanding.'

She didn't live to see the peace, but I'm sure her prayer for the uncertain first days of its existence helped all of us to begin the process of understanding. I think of her a lot on the feast of All Saints ... Which denomination will claim her in this church-going land? I'm sure she wouldn't want me to tell.

The ache of hope deferred

My uncle, who fought in World War I, was the first to introduce me to a country called Korea when war broke out there in 1950. War, from the safe distance of Ireland, was even exciting to a young boy as we placed the pins in the map where General McArthur landed at Inchon, or earlier, when town after town was swallowed up in the invasion from the north. A few years later, while studying theology, and war didn't seem such a great idea, I came across a book written by an Australian Columban Missionary whose parish was one of the first to fall in that war. On 25 June 1950, I was on my first summer holiday home from boarding school in Derry and, with that same old soldier uncle, was being introduced to pike fishing in Lough Erne in the north of Ireland. Father Crosbie, that Australian priest, opens his book, *Three Winters Cold*, with this short chapter:

Can you say off-hand how you spent Sunday June 25th 1950? Perhaps you find it hard to remember. For me, the events of that day are impossible to forget. On that date, at dawn, the armies of North Korea crossed the 38th parallel to begin their invasion of the south. I was caught up suddenly in the maelstrom of war; to spend anxious days awaiting what might come, knowing that the danger of sudden, violent death in that first sweep of the storm was very real; then to be made captive; to find myself thrust into a close-packed community of people who were, for the most part, strangers to one another and to me … a driven herd of bewildered folk with little in common, forced now to live in an intimacy far exceeding what would be tolerated even in a family; to endure with them the horrors of a death march; to be herded from place to place through months and years; to know the ache of hope deferred …

One September day in Seoul, I met the man who had survived that captivity where, for four years, he found himself one of the group of fifty civilian prisoners who had been herded together in conditions of abject misery, and who were forced to march the valley of the Yalu river in the winter of 1950, when the weak died and the stragglers were executed. They were Catholic, Anglican, Methodist and Salvation Army missionfolk who had come from America, England, Germany, Russia, Ireland, Australia and France.

Today, Phil Crosbie holds no bitterness for the dreadful experience but sees in it, rather, a deep lesson in tolerance and understanding. When faced with such suffering, there were no political arguments, no strident nationalism and no theological debates. He remembers with admiration the ageing Anglican Bishop Cooper, who worked with endless energy for the ailing French Carmelite nuns, and commissioner Lord of the Salvation Army, who acted with patience and good humour with all the group when hope was failing.

Father Crosbie, who seldom travels that death march even in memory, still finds endless inspiration in the memory of Nell Dyer, a Methodist from America, who was light, encouragement and hope to all who walked those dark, dark miles through the North Korean winter.

That evening I met him in Seoul, all those years later, it began to dawn on me that all of us on earth were on a march, a pilgrimage, and that, sometimes, that path was wrapped in the darkness. We too face days when war looms or where hunger strikes the desert land of Africa, days when the world we live in is being destroyed on land, in the oceans, and even in the atmosphere. Still we find time to raise flags of division, or dance around our tribal totem poles. Surely it doesn't need a global death march to convince us that we are, at heart, all brothers and sisters in need of each others' support.

Philip Crosbie is still on a mission at Kang Won Do, near the 38th parallel in Korea, still a line of division. He would like to go back to the Yalu river valley some day, to search for and mark the graves of his friends of all nations who died there, for he still greets every June 25th as a gift and life bonus from God.

Walter

I got my first French lesson from Walter, along a river bank high in the mountains of Co Tyrone, as he taught me how to fish in a trout-filled pool below the bridge of Glenhull. People at home, I later learned, thought that I was the one who heard all the terrible war secrets of the Somme, the trench battles in mud and blood. He had been there, and from the day he came home, had drawn a curtain of silence over the whole terrible event. All that surprised me, for the Walter I knew was the man who first opened my eyes to the magnificent detail of God's creation within the sweep of the hills around us. In return, I would read him the weekly newspaper for he had never mastered written English. He never went to church, but now and again he produced for me a small green leather-backed Bible, and would ask me to read at a page marked with a photograph of a soldier:

Then he said to his disciples:
'This is why I am telling you not to worry about your life and what you are to eat, nor about your body and how you are to clothe it. For life means more than food, and the body more than clothing. Think of the ravens. They do not sow or reap; they have no storehouses and no barns; yet God feeds them. And how much more are you worth than the birds! Can any of you, for all his worrying, add a single cubit to his span of life? If the smallest things, therefore, are outside your control, why worry about the rest? Think of the flowers: they never have to spin or weave. Yet I assure you, not even Solomon in all his regalia was robed like one of these. Now if this is how God clothes the grass in the field, which is there today and thrown into the furnace tomorrow, how much more will he look after you, men of little faith?'
Lk 12:22-28.

Jesus Christ must have been a poet, Walter would say, to have spoken words like that, and he must have had the eyes of a child who could see such simple things as if for the first time. The more I got to know the man, wounded by war, the more I realised that it was the poet in him that reached out to the Creator of the universe. One autumn evening, while he was whittling a branch with a fierce-looking penknife, he spoke about those days of pain in Belgium, about the Kemmel Hills and how, when he saw them, his mind went back to the Sperrin Hills of home. In the trudging days of mud and war he wondered if the rivers, the sandhills on the mountains of home, missed him and wondered where he was.

He told me about the churches and cathedrals lying in ruins in the wake of war, but his cathedral of the Owenkillew Valley was as majestic as when he left the gun and trench-coat behind him and came home. On spring days he would bring me to where wrens chattered among the stones, and to quiet sheltered rock faces where new life was coming to the wild flowers.

With the autumn he waited patiently to welcome back the wild geese and the winter wildlife. For Walter, the God creator of the universe, who had fixed the stars and called them by name, could never be a household name, could never be a household God limited to any man's hearth. War had desecrated men and destroyed the handiwork of God, and so it was, when Walter came home, he searched again for the sacredness of life in the eternal promise of every new spring, for it was there that he would find his God again.

During the eighties, the newspapers carried headlines about a mining company's discovery of gold in those hills. Only the local paper carried the simple few lines about Walter's death. As I came away from the graveyard, which was draped in the sad mellow colours of autumn, I realised that I had discovered the real riches of that land years ago, with the old battle-scarred soldier who had the bright eyes of a child.

Countdown

In the summer of 1995, if you crossed O'Connell Bridge in Dublin and looked down into the dark waters of the Liffey, you would have seen a strange timepiece which had already begun counting off the seconds until the turn of the century. It reminded me of the calendar I had stuck to the lid of my desk in the boarding school, with all its days marked off as the months made their weary way to the holidays at Christmas or summer. I'm sure there are many people who will have little nostalgia for the twentieth century, with its two world wars, its nuclear bombs and the irritating rashes of violence in many countries since. For all that, I didn't like the counting clock peeling off the millions of seconds one by one. It destroys the present, the now, today with all its opportunities. The Old Testament Book of Ecclesiastes reminds us:

> There is a season for everything,
> A time for every occupation under heaven.
> A time for giving birth, a time for dying,
> A time for planting, a time for uprooting what was planted,
> A time for killing, a time for healing,
> A time for knocking down, a time for building,
> A time for tears and a time for laughter,
> A time for mourning, a time for dancing,
> A time for throwing stones away, a time for gathering,
> A time for tearing and a time for sewing,
> A time for keeping silent and a time for speaking,
> A time for war and a time for peace.

Jesus Christ stressed, on more than one occasion, the importance of certain hours in all our lives – 'The hour,' he called it. His hour had not yet come, he said at Cana in Galilee when asked to do something to save the embarrassment of the newly married couple whose wine supply had run out. To you and to me continually comes the reminder that now is the acceptable hour. This day will never come our way again, and it's so easy to let it slip by in this endless rush to our next distraction. I remember reading somewhere a few lines of poetry which summed up the hurry of life:

Around around the sun we go
The moon goes round the earth
We do not die of death
We die of vertigo.

So many of our days pass as uneventful periods of twenty-four hours. In them we run the theme of nostalgia for the past and shaky hope for the future. We live for weekends and exist in the midweek preoccupations of life. Living like this makes of life a prison with short moments of parole. So often in our thinking we see miracles as happenings out of the ordinary, and that blinds us to the miracles and the gifts of this ordinary day. We must try to learn how to look on the present with possessive love. To be born again is to let the past go and look without condemnation upon the present. The fear or the anxiety that creep across our first moments of the new day, is not fear of the present but only of the past and future which do not exist. The past is gone, the future only rests in our imagination. An old friend of mine was quietly living out the last days of his long life in a hospice one night last winter. 'Looking back on my life, I didn't have too many red letter days, no dates that are carved into my memory,' he said. 'I wonder was my life a waste of time.' The sadness in his question was that he hadn't recognised how much peace, forgiveness, humour and concern he brought to all who knew him in all the seasons of their lives.

Casting cold eyes

On an autumn day some years ago, I went down the desert road from Jerusalem to Jericho. I remember it had two lanes of traffic then and I got to thinking if anyone was unlucky to get mugged, like the unfortunate man in Christ's parable, he would scarcely have been noticed from the fast moving, air-conditioned, pilgrim bus. The only casualty I noticed that evening was the remains of a rusted tank, a relic of victory or defeat from a previous war. The road, however, which Jesus spoke about, passes your front door and mine and we walk down it every day.

A man was once on his way down from Jerusalem to Jericho and fell into the hands of bandits; they stripped him, beat him and then made off, leaving him half dead. Now a priest happened to be travelling down the same road, but when he saw the man, he passed by on the other side. In the same way a Levite who came to the place saw him, and passed by on the other side. But a Samaritan traveller who came on him was moved with compassion when he saw him. He went up to him and bandaged his wounds, pouring oil and wine on them. He then lifted him onto his own mount and took him to an inn and looked after him.
Lk 10:30-35, *NJB*.

This day, I'm sure, looks like another busy one. There is the work which you will have to take home with you, there are all the preoccupations in what we call modern living, and we keep telling each other that we have no time left for visiting or looking up the friends of yesterday. The day will leave us drained of energy and millions of us will, at the end of the day, sit and stare at canned synthetic entertainment because we are too weary to think or do anything else.

With all that pressure, we haven't the time to notice those who are lying wounded at the side of the Jerusalem-Jericho road, which passes your front door and mine and which we will walk down any day. There they are, the men and women who have been robbed of family pride, self confidence or their good name. They lie there wounded by endless months without work, or by a fast moving world which makes little allowance for those who can't keep up to its pace. Christians have been defined as people responsible for others, yet in this work I find myself sometimes being very enthusiastic about letting others be the eyes for the blind, ears for the deaf, shelter for the homeless and food for the starving. Its easier to telephone a few pounds of support to *Children In Need* than to get engaged in voluntary support locally. It's easier to give to the anonymous poor in distant Africa than to help at a local night shelter. We will support enthusiastically the campaign for the mentally handicapped child, but we leave them out of the guest lists at our birthday or wedding celebrations.

We walk down the road of life and hope that it won't be too cluttered and, for the life of me, in searching through the teaching of Jesus Christ, I can't find the words that tell me that the work of caring is for the select few.

The road from Jerusalem to Jericho passes anywhere through these islands and we walk down it everyday. I wonder now and again, how will you and I be remembered by those who survive us when we have walked it for the last time. Will we be remembered as the people who stopped and cared, or could someone justifiably scribble on our headstones (with apologies to the Irish Poet W.B. Yeats):

'they cast a cold eye on life and on death –
and passed by.'

The Cap

I remember his cap
shaped for eighty seasons
to his tousled head.
An oval plastic crown, darkened by blobs of brylcream
at occasional wakes and weddings
half hid the makers name
in Nottingham.
He always found it where he threw it
on the rare hours it got its freedom.
Even in death they stayed together
for the heart attack took him gently
as he lay back on the haystack
when the final fatigue slumped
his weary legs on a summer Sperrin field.
The shapeless cap has stayed
plastic-wrapped on a corner shelf
beside his picture
snapped when the Americans came in fifty-seven.
Not an heirloom, but a relic now
for on it, he, bare-headed, dropped on one knee every Sunday
to honour his God without liturgical fuss
just inside
the backdoor of Cranagh church.

Broken Strings

At the auction
after the priest's funeral
he got the fiddle for a bargain.
And in the winter's nights
he played duets with the whingeing wind
in the stone dry barn
until the day he ventured
a hornpipe and a reel
at John Fada's wedding.
And down the years the fiddled tunes
lilted the joys of harvest and homecoming
or sobbed a slow lament
in the silence of the barn again.
But no lament was teased by any bow
when death diverted him
at the crossroads on a winter's night.
The breast-pressed horn
shrilled away his life
across the frost frilled fields.
A broken fiddle hung by one spared string
on a hawthorn bush
which would bear no berries again.

The Ecclesiastical Inspector

Tony never liked the Catechism
for his mind was focused
on football teams
which wore the colours of the county
or the local green and white
of Carrickbeg.

The diocesan examiner,
humourless and tired with his task
came every May
to praise Helen Mary, the teacher's girl
and the McGurk twins
who knew the prayers better than
their granny.

Mrs McGlynn, severe and strained
could only hope that Tony
would not repeat the heresy of last year
when he disentangled
four gods from the mystery.

As Tony stood before the summer inquisition
he spotted the golden retriever
in the inspector's car
and turned the conversation.

The priest relaxed and put aside the book
'Did Jesus have a dog, Tony?'

'No Father, for it would have been there at Calvary.'
He went home proudly pocketing a ten shilling note.
Helen Mary and the McGurk twins
felt no justice
in religion.

In God's good time

On an October day, I stood at the graveside of an old friend. The air was still, for autumn had stolen in over Donegal. He had lived a rich fulfilled life as a priest. Sickness had slowed and aged him and a stroke some years ago left him brittle. Then, suddenly, in the autumn of his life, death came as twilight fell on the shortening day. As we stood around the grave, the leaves kept dropping to earth as their season too came to an end. There is a certain sadness about the mellow days of October. The flowers sense the coming winter; the trees give up their splendid green finery. The promise of spring gave way to the extravagance of summer and now autumn, ever so gently, prepares nature for the stark days of winter death. The story of our lives is reflected in the endless changing of the seasons. There was the sap of new life in our childhood days when we ran down lanes of joy or played with friends in what seemed the endless days of yesterday. We flourished in the summer of new commitments, new homes and new families, and then, with the signs of greying maturity and blurring vision, we discover all too soon that the autumn of our lives has brought its stillness and the possibility of peace. Then, like winter, death will come with its colourless days of grief.

Beyond my window there is a rowan tree. It was late that year before it gave away its leaves and winter gave it the look of death ... and when I thought it would have to be uprooted in April, it suddenly sprung to life again.

A Christian people know in their hearts that, just as the seasons move on, and just as surely as spring follows winter, however

28

severe, so a new life begins for those we lose in seeming death. In the funeral liturgy for my friend the phrase 'Life is changed, not ended' told me something of his new life, his new spring in a more fertile setting than earth. Earth, for all its beauty is a barren place, for, as I left the leaf-strewn cemetery and turned on the car radio for the midday news, the main bulletin was of another untimely death … a green leaf nipped by cruelty in the spring of his life, and I thought in sadness about those who disrupt God's perfect timing and bring days of frozen grief to families all over this province, who want nothing but to celebrate the spring or summer of their loved ones' lives.

The flowers will blossom again. The tree will display the green buds of spring. The fresh berries will come again on the blackthorn. The chrysalis will become the butterfly … all in God's good time. But isn't there something pathetically pitiful when any man decides to interrupt the eternal plan of God and end a human life completely out of its season?

Out of focus

He came out of the small farmhouse into the bright sunlight of a late August evening. His once powerful frame was supported by a son and daughter who fought back the tears as they walked slowly to the waiting car. This was the day they had dreaded for months, the day when they could no longer give him the proper care and nursing support. The illness had stolen over him after his wife's death. In the beginning he gave the names of the dead to the visiting neighbours, but corrected himself by laughing off the mistake. Then the immediate past was lost in details of war years and the cigarettes which he insisted came from Turkey.

Uncharacteristically, he embraced his son before easing himself into the front seat of the car. For a moment he gazed out blankly on the fields he had tilled for fifty years. He looked at the sycamore tree behind the barn and his eyes seemed to have focused in recognition for a few seconds before the glazed look stole over them again. The car moved down the leafy lane on its journey to the nursing home in the town which had all the facilities for coping with Alzheimer's disease.

His son, driving distractedly, knew that his father was now just the remains of greatness – his memory, deep frozen, which all the loving care of the previous six months did little to thaw. Lines from the poet, Brendan Kennelly came flooding into his mind:

No sooner downstairs after the night's rest
And in the door
Than you started to dance a step
In the middle of the kitchen floor.

And as you danced
You whistled.
You made your own music
Always in tune with yourself.

Well, nearly always, anyway.
You're buried now
In Lislaughlin Abbey
And whenever I think of you
I go beyond the old man
Mind and body broken
To find the unbroken man.
It is the moment before the dance begins.

(*Selected Poems* – Brendan Kennelly, Kerrymount Publications, 18, Fitzwilliam Square, Dublin 2)

Weeks later, I went to see him. He was sitting in the garden of the nursing home, wrapped up against the hint of autumn in the evening breeze. He stared at me, striving for recognition – but none came.

Around him the roses were still in bloom as the old man withered. A day or two later, he reached out for the accordion when the local band came in to entertain, and when his fingers caught the occasional chord, the hint of a smile stole back.

This simple incident provided a great deal of comfort to his son and daughter and to his grandchildren. They remembered him play the melodeon at weddings, long before the acoustic groups took over, and they recalled the dancing at home on the kitchen floor as he beat out the rhythm with his massive hob-nail boots. His tunes began to come back to them, and they were the key to all he had given them in those long and happy years. Sometimes he wandered away from the carefully groomed gardens of the nursing home, and went into the visiting area where he would sit on the children's swings and try to find some lost rhythm of the lost years of childhood. His own grandchildren would try to push him gently, but he stared at them unsmilingly and they withdrew in fear. They would then take him by both hands and lead him to the garden. As his son watched him, he remembered other days when his sister and he went into the mountains with their father. He always took them by the hand when the path became uncertain. Now, in his final days, through the kindness of those who nursed him, God, they thought, was taking the hand of their stumbling father and guiding him to a heaven where memories would be restored again.

Wings over war

The first light snow of winter had dusted the Glenelly Valley here in the mountain parish in Northern Ireland where I was the parish priest. Behind me, Sawel mountain, the highest Sperrin peak, was already wreathed in snow. I was making my way down the valley on a cold Sunday morning, when I spotted this large brown bird gliding above me with the slow lazy flapping of its broad wings. 'It's a small world, Father,' shouted a man from a nearby field, 'the last time I saw a buzzard was when I was working in Saudi Arabia.' 'It made me think of home then,' he went on, 'but then, God's hints at heaven are everywhere.' Those same hints are touched on by the Russian writer, Dostoevsky:

> Love all God's creation, the whole and every grain of sand in it. Love every leaf, every ray of God's light. Love the animals, love the plants, love everything. If you love everything, you will perceive the divine mystery in things. Once you perceive it you will begin to comprehend it better every day, and you will come at last to love the whole world with an all-embracing love.

That Sunday morning, the desert sands of Saudi were bristling with the machinery of war, for the Gulf War had begun. For days the warm deserts filled our television screens with armies pawing the sand for war, while the night skies were lit up with exploding flares as the training for battle progressed. It was no place for buzzards with lazy wings. The migrating birds, who knew the beauty of the sand desert with its reddish dunes sculptured by the wind, must have winged on as they saw the earth throw up its dust in the wake of rumbling tanks. Looking across the world from the relatively peaceful pastoral setting of the valley, the prophecy of Isaiah

seemed as far away as ever: 'The desert shall rejoice and bloom like the rose,' were his words. There was little rejoicing in the desert of Saudi, Kuwait or Iraq while the arguments for war were up for debate. Still, in this valley, where the first frosts caught us, we too had our war which had been festering for over twenty years without the high drama of desert frontiers. That morning in church we had been declaring our loyalty to Christ who showed a lost desert folk a way out of the wilderness, by telling them that he was the way, the truth and the light. Soft words of grace he spoke unto a lost desert folk who listened wondering.

So my mind went back to the buzzard again and to a weaving flight of starlings who swept and turned in the blue crisp morning, and I remembered a line from an American writer:

The whole world and all creatures will be to you nothing else than an open book and a living Bible in which you may study, without any previous instruction, the science of God and from which you may learn his will.

Maybe we have dulled ears for the words of God, maybe our eyes are glazed by neon lights or endless images on television. Maybe we should open our eyes and look again on the earth and its beauty and ponder on its silent message. If we have nothing but a Christian stance, we have no right to sit in judgement on those who misread the Bible or the Koran and who face each other in battle on the other side of the world.

'Every creature is a word of God and is a book about God,' wrote the Flemish Mystic, Meister Eckhart, and out on the Glenelly Valley I saw the truth of it. You could catch the care of God watching the shepherd carry an early lamb to the warmth of the house. The migrating swans from Iceland gave a hint that God still cared for us for they flew west with their high cry echoing for miles, and even the dead sparrow lying frozen on the ground was noted by God who kept telling us that we, human beings, were of much more importance. Still, important people, in the eyes of God, that morning were facing each other with death – on the burning sands of Saudi and Iraq, where not even the high-flying buzzard might be safe.

Funeral, Ballykelly

Another day, another dawn over this island home of ours, and too many people are rising from broken sleep to face a day of emptiness in the wake of the violence which has stolen so many away. Over three thousand dead and not enough days in any year to accommodate them with their own anniversaries! Another day, another dawn, and in a few short hours the silent shifting of feet begins again along the waters of the Foyle to the graveyards of Faughanvale, Ballykelly and Tullynee. Churches were never built for funerals like these, so neighbours, head bowed in quiet grief, will stand around and listen to the voice of priest and minister calling again for Christian peace, tolerance, forgiveness and mercy. Are these voices crying in the wilderness of a land where cruel and distorted violence has withered the green shoots of hope and goodwill?

The deep, dark waters of the Foyle have seen pain often before when young people took the tender from the Quayside at Derry for the emigrant ship anchored off Moville. They went away – never to come back. The last few weeks have stolen away the young again, alongside those in the summer or autumn of their lives.

November is a month of dying, for the promise of spring is now in the faded falling leaf. In it we set our All Souls' Day and Remembrance Sunday. Around the London Cenotaph and war memorials, people will stand and remember the uniformed victims of war. But today, and over the last weeks, we have been remembering the victims of war who swore no loyalties, donned no uniform, marched to no battlefield. In this war the fallen, for the most part, are men and women, boys and girls who dreamt of nothing but a future peace, and their remembrance days will chill those who survived them for life.

Can Roisin Cairns ever celebrate her birthday again, when the memory of shots, which she believed to be a Halloween prank, robbed her of her brothers, or how can the family and friends of Leanne Murray of the Shankhill ever face her birthday again without her gentle presence, or will Halloween ever be celebrated in Greysteel because the angel of death gate-crashed their celebration of life?

Sadly, violence grows wild here because, unwittingly, we have given it a fertile soil. For too long we have sat around our campfires and traded myths. We have told fiction as fact, rumour as truth and doubt as dogma. We have blared our anthems, planted our flags and even tried to enlist God to shore up our own versions of orthodoxy. Our defiant drumbeats have dulled our ears, and we can't hear the endless cry for peace. Maybe even today, in the silence of the shuffling feet, we might begin to hear the pain of a people whose main ambition is to live.

Another day, another dawn ... But for too many, the day is already shrouded in darkness.

Christmas child

You couldn't have failed to notice her in the school playground on a sharp December day. A crown of enthusiastic supporters from her own class counted her skips at yelling level. In the middle of the circle she stayed to the task, her black hair bouncing on slender shoulders, her breath gasps visible in the cold city air as the number crept towards two hundred, the sponsored target for the starving children of Ethiopia. Yet I knew that, with the coming of the school Christmas holiday, the adulation, the colour of excitement, would all evaporate for her and her younger brother.

The previous Christmas day she had come to the early Mass with her brother of five and told the priest that Santa had forgotten to come to them. The sad reality was that he was still in bed, confused with the alcohol and the effervescent tablets that failed to still the beating in his head and the turmoil in his stomach. It had been like that for years every Christmas. Santa Claus had been mother for a number of years, before she got tired trying to reform her husband and joined him in drinking through the Christmas season. That Christmas day, the priest brought them in for breakfast and told them a story about Santa being delayed because of demands from the poorer, starving children in far off Africa. He arranged for a Santa to call, from a family who had the hired robes, and the children both showed total amazement at how he knew they were there having breakfast in this unusual Christmas morning setting.

By the time they got home, their enthusiasm and joy caught both parents unaware, and their excitement was totally alien to both father and mother, who supped two coffee cups and with each sip returned to the grey reality of a December morning which happened to be Christmas day. And with the growing realisation must have come guilt, because anger took over and the teddy bear and the toy truck where snatched and thrown into the bin, as he declared to all the street that he was no pauper and wasn't depending on any charity. Some neighbouring children, whose parents knew the sad emptiness of the home, called and asked them to join them in playing with their new toys, only to be met by a father who seemed alien to the joy and peace of the season. Later the little girl would tell the teacher that the mother rescued the teddy and the truck when the father left the house in the evening, and that she had hugged the teddy into a deep sleep before the television which robbed her of another Christmas day.

The Christmas feast of the Holy Innocents, celebrated each year in the wake of the Nativity, seems always to be about a massacre in Bethlehem, all those years ago when the Christ was born. But the celebration of the birth of Christ each year seems to throw up the mental massacre of too many children, too many innocents, who don't necessarily starve for food in the dusty fields of famine, but starve for acceptance and love where peace and goodwill are supposed to abound.

The nowness of everything

'I came home to die,' he told me when I met him one autumn morning at Dublin airport. The honesty and sense of finality in his greeting shocked me, for I was meeting a young man, not yet thirty, whom I had known as a student and successful journalist who had gone to Philadelphia to widen his experience. In mid-summer he had paid little attention to his loss of appetite, putting it all down to the virus of overwork, late hours and snatched meals. Then a consultant in hospital told him gently that his life was to be measured in months. Over the weeks I watched him, waiting for the anger and the wild bargaining with his God but, instead, he became a man of deep inner peace born, he told me, of his discovery of the beauty of his native valley and the real warmth of neighbours whose rural ways he might have despised if the illness hadn't focused his vision. He had found the beauty that the writer Dennis Potter had experienced months before him:

> I'm almost serene, I can celebrate life.
> Below my window there's an apple tree in blossom.
> It's white.
> And looking at it – instead of saying,
> 'Oh, that's a nice blossom' –
> now, looking at it through the window,
> I see the whitest, frothiest, blossomest blossom
> that there ever could be.
> The nowness of everything is absolutely wondrous.
> If you see the present tense – boy, do you see it,
> and boy, do you celebrate it.

(Dennis Potter in his last interview with Melvyn Bragg on Channel 4)

Perhaps too many of us sleepwalk through life. Jesus Christ did draw our attention to eyes that see not and ears that hear not. The advertiser has stood on tip-toe for years now and beamed his neon distractions at us. Others entice us to believe only in what they see as important, and so we rush to buy things we can't afford, to impress people we don't particularly like.

The household portrayed on the television advertisement has no poverty, no breakdowns, no cot deaths and no cancer. The multi-coloured world of nature, which became the adventure place of my friend, has lost its attraction. Still, this young man spent that autumn exploring the gradual surrender of summer's beauty to the first hint of November's frost. In that he saw his own gentle surrender of vitality as smooth and inevitable, and as beautiful as the golden days of his last autumn. These days he lived to the full. He regretted the time lost which could have been used to know and appreciate the love and unobtrusive generosity of his family and friends, and how little he had appreciated the words of Hopkins:

The world is charged with the grandeur of God.
It will flame out like shining from shook foil.

He told me that in the dying season of his own life, he felt that he was like a canoeist who had thrown away his paddle and let the fast flow-ing river take him – 'maybe that's what trust in God is,' he went on.

In the words of the Irish poet, Kavanagh, whose book of collected poems was his constant companion, he prayed that he would still be alive when 'April's ecstacy danced in every white thorn tree' – but it was not to be.

He died on a January morning when the first flecks of snow blew in with an east wind. To all who knew him, he left a legacy of the open eye and the listening ear, and the ability to read death and resurrec-tion in the ever-changing seasons.

October 14th 1994:
The day that peace broke out

It was an early June morning some years ago that I met an old French farmer wheeling his bicycle near the beach at Arromanches in Normandy. 'What do you remember,' I asked him, 'of that June day of the Normandy invasion, when the allied troops landed with shells and gunfire raging all along the beach below us?' 'I remember,' he said, 'the day the war moved from here. I still remember the sudden peace, the singing of the birds and the cry of the gulls.'

This morning I heard the birds singing early, and the stillness of the misty dawn was, for me, the symbol of the peace that is almost tangible here after almost a quarter century of death and decimation. But alongside the blessing of peace, I felt the twinge of pain for all those whose lives had fallen away like the frost-nipped leaves which drifted down over this valley for the past few days. Some of these days a political commentator will tell us the cost of human life of this regional conflict. The cemeteries will mark the days of death in granite all over this small Province.

But this is just the dawn of a new day and a new era of hope and endless possibilities. What the day holds in store for us is what we make of it. Ceasefires bring silence, and a time to hear the gentle cry or the muffled sobbing of those who have been heart broken by the angel of death, who was directed to them at the whim of some human being.

Peace is a beautiful dawning this morning, but the day will be what we make of it.

The energy that went into the war will have to go into the peace.
Jesus declared that blessedness will be with the peacemaker, not the
peace lover. There will be no blessedness for those who might sit
back, relax and wait for a handful of politicians to pick up the pieces
of this jigsaw and put it together for good.

The people who feel happy this morning, in not having ever raised
a fist in anger for all the days and years of the war, are now asked to
lift a hand for peace, or lend a hand to the many voluntary agencies
who want to heal the wounds and bind up the searing sores of so
many. There are too many hidden scars, too many deep wells of
revenge and bitterness, and they call out for the healing hand.
Stress has slipped in between too many husbands and wives and
has stolen love away. The healing hand of the Christ can only reach
out through the flesh and blood of those who offer their hands to
Christ the peacemaker. Yes, we must bring a greater energy to
peace than that brought into the war which died at midnight.

This autumn morning, with its mellow sadness, is just to the beginning. The war has moved on. If you and I become the peacemakers,
which we are called to be by Jesus Christ, then we will be blessed by
God and by a generation of children who, like the old French man,
will have time again to listen to the birds and the cry of the gulls.

The Clown

Sometime after ten
the flaps were pulled aside on the circus tent
in Tommy Mooney's upper field
and wide-eyed children faced the darkness
gripping tight to parents' hands and treading
on the slatted boards across the mud
to find the car and home to bed.
And all the way back they talked at fever pitch
about the clown
and tried to catch his shriek of joy
or the shoulder rolling of his tousled head.
Next day at school
their ambition stopped at the red nosed fool
who let their spirits soar above
the gathering days of winter darkness.
In Madge's post office, which housed the only parish phone,
I saw the clown, defrocked that very day
trying number after number on the black wall phone
with its starting handle to alert the exchange in Omagh.
She would tell me later that he was searching for his wife
who ran away the day before
with the serious little man who sat in the caravan near Mooney's
gate
collecting the tickets to see the circus
and the clown.

Chilly waters of isolation

She had lovingly shaped the clay into a flowerpot only after repeated failures. Into every detail on the glazing and the painting she had put all her energy, for this was her wedding present to her sister. She wrapped it, tied it with a bow, and offered it with pride the evening the bride-to-be called at Emmaus House. But the day of the wedding she spent with the rest of her friends in the centre for the handicapped at Kwang-Ju, South Korea, for she had got no invitation to the celebration. I was visiting the centre that day, and the words of an Irish writer reached across the world to me:

You are not the child they were expecting.
No – she was to be strong. Not like you
with your unconforming ways and words,
Embracing all you meet, even strangers.
Heedless to all the dangers.

Sour disappointment after such a hopeful wait.
Not the promise of eager expectant days.
What went wrong? Had there been some mistake?
You cry to make them see – show understanding
of what your presence is demanding.

Daily you drag yourself from blissful sleep
and dress in garments of patient suffering,
wash in the chilly waters of isolation.
Ready to forgive seventy times seven – show concern.
Hoping they will learn.
(J. V. McCarron, unpublished poem)

That morning, Anna Kim had certainly washed in the chilly waters of isolation but, within the hour, she felt enveloped again in the love of that house which had been founded by a Columban Missionary from Ireland, Noel O'Neill. He had gone out there in 1957 in the aftermath of the Korean War, to Kwang-Ju, only miles away from the town of Mokpo where three men from the same mission had been captured during the war, never to be seen again. From the beginning, he had been involved in a beggars' camp where he first met the handicapped who held no place in Korean society then. These people, the Chong Shin Chi Che Cha, 'the slow minded' as they were called, became his chief task and his first love. In the confuscian tradition, the learned person won respect, so the children born with any thought defect were discretely kept aside.

That September day, thirty years later, he brought me to see his three centres, where the handicapped are loved and reverenced by local Korean helpers, who have already seen and sensed the real wisdom in these seemingly backward children and adults. The inscribed stone in the entrance to Emmaus House sums up the philosophy and the Christian attitude to all who come here:

Integration rather than segregation.
Independence sooner that dependence.
Acceptance in place of rejection.
Respect rather than pity.

Noel O'Neill had the experience of working with the people of Jean Vanier's L'Arche movement in Canada and in London, and here in Kwang-Ju I sensed the same love, caring and joy. The young adults, who form the team, never welcome any handicapped person so as to salve their consciences, but because they want help them their freedom for they are accepted with their limitations as well as their abilities. There too I discovered that language was no barrier to communication.

Their language was in their beautiful gestures of welcome, their smiles of recognition and in their tears when it was time to say goodbye.

If Anna Kim had washed in the chilly waters of isolation that morning, while her sister celebrated a love pledged in a marriage ceremony, she soon experienced the other dimension of love in a priest and people pledged to serve Jesus Christ in the least of his brothers and sisters, the least, that is, in the measuring tape of this world.

Wage packet

The newscasts of the week were so predictable, grim and gruesome that I decided to give the news a miss that night. The silence of the house was disturbed by a single phonecall just after nine.

Friends of mine in the north of London had been out celebrating something as simple as a first wage packet. When their eldest son came home one Friday night four years before, full of pride with his own hefty cheque from his first wage as an electronics engineer, I was invited along to a popular restaurant to celebrate, and I watched his father clasp his wife's hand as their son picked up the bill and signed his cheque in a flurry of confidence.

On a June night, years later, they were out again and it was from the Burger King they phoned me. Maria had brought them out to celebrate, with less luxury, because she had got her first pay from the Leisure Centre. The money was less, the achievement greater, for Maria is a Down's Syndrome girl of eighteen who overcame misunderstanding, misplaced sympathy and isolation, to that evening of quiet celebration. That night the joy was infectious, as her parents spoke before handing the phone to her for a few monosyllabic words of excitement.

She was born in silence. She never cried and the nurses were slow to speak lest their words would betray what their trained eyes thought they saw. It was Maria's colour that confirmed months of suspicion and fear when her mother took her in her arms for her first frail encounter. People meant well when they came to see her when she came home from hospital, but platitudes about her spe-

cial child made Maria more an alien with no hopes, no future and
no bright horizons.

But hope began to grow and, with the years, Maria uncovered the
strength of all her family. They had to watch as she fought for
recognition and friendship in a world that was geared for financial
success and security. They watched their son struggle for the A-levels
that would be his key to that world, while she asked only to love
and be loved, to respect and be respected, to acquire only to give
away.

Her mother once told me that Maria had been touched by death at
birth, but on a hot summer's day in London, when she pulled away
from her father's guiding and protecting hand and ran up to an old
woman on the steps of St Martin in the Fields and offered her a half
licked ice cream, both her parents knew that she was a life-giver,
even if her own womb would never carry new life. From then on,
their encouragement towards her independence was the reason,
I'm sure, for that first proud pay day celebration.

I turned on the radio before I fell asleep. Prices quoted on the Tokyo
exchange were down, the pound was trading well against the dol-
lar and the FTSE index was a few points up at the close of the stock
exchange. I'm sure the news didn't put Maria off her sleep.

Closer Calvary

I was Joseph once
old before my time on the dusty road to Bethlehem
that took a short-cut across the stage
in a parish hall near Gortin.
And I didn't like Mary
and cared less if all the inns were full
for she was good at reading and writing
and arithmetic
and the master called her his favourite pupil
and sang her praises every day.
Sitting between the priest and the minister
from the grey church beyond the town
he froze me with a solemn stare
for I smirked when Mary
lost the doll redeemer
and sniffling infant angels missed their cue.

But at that memory I smile no more
for that same Mary lost a son on a closer calvary
here in Ireland
where Jesus is mislaid again and again
in the endless killing fields.

Nativity Play

Mary of Nazarath
married to your neighbour, Joseph,
who worked with wood and nails.
Did it ever cross your mind
in busy Bethlehem
between the spasms of pain that drained your face
as He, the Christ, womb curled, moved towards birth,
that a little one in Ireland
would dress in blue
and take the reluctant hand of a neighbour boy
to steer him to a stable
and find a crib
on a light-drenched stage in Castletown?
And I sit and watch in this darkened hall
and wonder how will she remember this night
when the acting ends
and the drama of life
finds her, some winter night,
birth pained
with no applause.

Dispensary (Greencastle 1944)

A racking cough tore at my ribs
and father cursed in fretful sleep
muttered about Friday's dispensary
and the TB on her side of the house.

The blue oil stove on the flagstone floor
breathed fumes to kill the cold.
Worried women with delicate children needing malt
swapped symptoms
and ten acred mountain farmers, lungs smoke caught
cursed Tuesday's budget and the price of Woodbine.

Tuned to my heart, he tapped my back with finger hammer
and to antiphons of 'cough, lad, cough'
found 'twas nothing but a chest made delicate
by months of winter to be cured from the brown bottle
in measured spoons.

In the church on the way home to a day off school
my father knelt in quiet prayer
and left two candles flickering for God
who had kept it, God bless the mark,
away from us.

Doneraile

The sodden churchyard, grey with death,
spoke not of joy or life-shocked newness that
sullen summer day in Doneraile.
Stoney sentences, as short as life, marked consumption's
gallop down lanes of family loving.
This was no place of resurrection, I sought the dying with the
dead.
And then she opened soft-cupped hands, unlined by
suffering sores at seven,
and let the winged colour
of the butterfly free
then pointed to a furry fledgling on a hidden graveyard nest
with all the vastness of the Cork blue sky, aching in his wings.
Again, the girl child was first to the tomb,
to shout of resurrection.

The Shoehorn

She took it home from a gypsy stall at Gortin Fair
and spent the dark winter night
teaching himself, in the full mantle whiteness
of the Tilly Lamp
to slide the heavily stockinged foot
into the hob-nailed boot.
'It would fit them better if they came up
with something for pulling off the wellingtons'
he kept repeating
as the bottles of stout, a surprise every fair day
since before the war
gave words to his vanishing patience.
Next morning, roused by the barking dog
hours before dawn
he slipped on the boot with the big spoon
from the drawer
in the kitchen table.

Autumn Churchyard

Do not search for me down among the marble headstones
where rooks on November branches
make gathering cry for the dying year.
Do not look for me where summer's leaves
decay on graves of winter grass.
Do not imagine me as last you saw me
pale, bruised and empty of life.
I am not here –
but see that shaft of sunlight
which spots the grey dark lake of late November
on the heather hillside of Donegal
or listen to the thrush
squeeze out the last notes of its sunny summer song
or hear the laughter
I splashed in my sister's face
on the sun drenched beach that summer before I left you.
I go on playing not where winter withers
but where spring
Is eternal.

Birthdays

My precious little child
Your grandmother died on the day
that she was born
with a gentle gap of seventy years.
I cried her to the grave
and into the months beyond.
What would she have made of you
dying on your birthday
with only a breathless gap
of two short hours?

Departing swans

The whooper swans in the valley below had been restless for days. The wild call of the Arctic had been heard, but they were still loath to leave the fields of Ireland to make that majestic flight back to their breeding grounds. They would all settle back and the April fields were white again. Another disturbance and they rose in hundreds and their high call echoed all the way up the valley to where Agnes sat at the window watching. She sat at the window most of the day since the arthritis confined her, and she passed the day talking to God in prayer, with an intermittent word now and again to the budgie whose cage gave him a clearer view of the valley and fields below. A daily help prepared the little she ate and moved her to the 'settled bed', as she called it, beside the fireplace when darkness closed in. The house was content with the furnishing of half a century ago when she came there as a young bride. The settled bed was where she gave birth to five sons, all of whose pictures of youthful days were ranged across the mantelpiece. They had gone long since when they found that the land wasn't generous and demanded too much pain and too little profit. She talked about them all the time to the home help, even though everybody knew that, apart from a card at Christmas, they had lost all contact with her. It was all so different from the days when she explored the rugged beauty of the glen with the five boys, in the years after their father died from tuberculosis. The youngest told her one day that sitting with her looking down on Lough Swilly from Altmore mountain was what he took heaven to be – but that was years before.

Is it true that after this life of ours we shall one day be awakened by a terrifying clamour of trumpets?

Forgive me, God, but I console myself that the beginning and resurrection of all of us dead will simply be announced by the crowing of the cock.
After that we'll remain lying down a while…
The first to get up will be Mother …
We'll hear her quietly laying the fire,
Quietly putting the kettle on the stove
And cosily taking the teapot out of the cupboard.
We'll be home once more.

(Vladimir Holan 1905-1980, translated by George Theiner)

They were doing well, she would assure any of us who called, and
she listed off the streets in New York, Philadelphia, Chicago and
Perth where they lived, with the same ease as she would answer
Catechism classes of seventy years before. But deep down, the loneliness crippled her worse than the arthritis. She waited every
Christmas week for the mail and every Christmas one or two of the
sons would disappoint her – but the cards she got still sat in the
windowsill until St Patrick's Day. She would make excuses for
them in their neglect, and went on watching the visiting swans
from October until the late spring every year. She spoke knowl-
edgeably about their migration and about the miracle of finding
these fields year after year, and of their support for each other. The
boys, she would tell us, grew up with the yearly migration, and that
the memory of the valley was still alive with them in Long Island or
Bustleton Avenue.

The neighbours who sat with her on a late April evening some
years ago, said that she hummed a nostalgic farewell to the swans
the evening they lifted and struck out North from Ireland to the
Arctic. Somehow, she knew, she wouldn't see them return. She
wouldn't allow the neighbours to send for her sons, even if the
addresses could be found, the evening she knew that she had heard
the call from God. 'Just put my death notice in the paper and add
American and Australian papers please copy,' she whispered.

Someone at the evening funeral said that the night the Whooper
Swans went back, the budgie chirped like never before. I don't
think that any of the migrating swans heard the caged bird's plain-
tive song.

Waiting is hard to endure...

The season of Advent, in the Christian calendar, has many themes. The one which appeals to me every year is the theme of waiting. Maybe it's because I'm an impatient man who won't order any item in a store, queue for tickets, or arrive ten minutes early to my dentist and be forced to read his well-thumbed magazines in nervous anticipation. My neighbour, Herbie over the river, is worse. He has a set day in November for having the garden cleared of fallen leaves and he has been known to shake two stubborn trees violently for holding their few withered leaves beyond the fall-by-date. In this sense, he is not an advent man. Too often we give the impression that we have nothing to wait for because we have Jesus, the Messiah, safely enclosed in our denomination. That's why the words of Paul Tillich challenge me every December.

> I think of the churchman who does not wait for God because he possesses him, enclosed in an institution. I think of the believer who does not wait for God, because he possesses him, enclosed within his own experience.
> I am convinced that much of the rebellion against Christianity is due to the overt or veiled claim of the Christian to possess God, and therefore, also, to the loss of this element of waiting so decisive for the prophets.
> They did not possess God, they waited for him.

(Paul Tillich, *The Boundaries of our Being*)

Advent is a time of waiting. We wait for birth, for love and for life itself to reveal its meaning and purpose. We wait for the spring-sown seed to reveal its green freshness in summer, and then we wait for the harvest. Nothing worthwhile in life is sudden. Some Christian people, in this season, sing out their Advent liturgy in anticipation of the second coming of Christ. For others, calling themselves Christian, Christ may not have come home to them for the first time. Advent is about waiting in hope. It's the same waiting in hope of the mother to be. It's the hope that supported Mary on that tiresome road to Bethlehem and the seeming lack of concern of God for his son's mother. To hope, I suppose, is to be ready for that which is not yet born.

Here, in Northern Ireland, we still wait. We wait for the coming of Jesus as prince of peace because, while many do think he has come, the prophecies of Isaiah are not fulfilled here. The swords have not been hammered into plough shares, nor the spears into sickles, and still they train for war.

Our silent night is shattered by waiting sirens, and sorrow will squat in too many homes at Christmas. Maybe it's because, unlike advent people who look to the future, we remain rooted in the past. We have litanies and dates of where battles were won and lost, where blood offerings were made in the name of God – and he would have none of it and, lest we forget, we parade the date and the event on banners behind bands, or sprayed on walls by people whose memory doesn't go back to the Beatles. Albert Schweitzer once wrote that the energy in the world is equal to the hope in it, and even if only a few people share such hopes, a power is created which nothing can hold down. Maybe we Christian people should wait again in hope for the birth of a peace conviction in us, that would be underlined and authenticated by the Messiah who was called 'wonder counsellor – prince of peace', and would, with us, usher in the coming of a new humanity.

Life line

Kate was always glad when Christmas was over. The commercial selling of the season, which came earlier each year, did nothing but underline the emptiness she felt as her home remained without a child after ten years of marriage. She could remember the magic of the morning when she was a child herself, and would recall her mother's words that there was no proper Christmas without children. It was hard for her to focus in on the child in the Bethlehem cave while the white-laced crib, inherited from her mother, lay empty. Now and again she fought back the bitterness that welled up in her when she saw any young women struggle with an unwanted or unplanned pregnancy while her womb remained empty. Her faith in the creator God seemed weaker each year. Then she found an echo of her deepest feelings in an old prayer poem of the thirteenth century, translated from the Irish:

Blessed Trinity pity me
You can give the blind man sight
Put growing grass in any rock
Give our house a child this night.

You colour the woods with blossoms bright
Is there anything you cannot do?
The branches sprout their silken leaves
What's a little child to you?

Corn from blades and oak from acorn
Miracles of life awake.
Harvest from a fist of seedlings
Is a child so hard to make?

It dawned on her one day that her life had become an endless round of consultant's waiting rooms in an effort to prove to herself and her husband that no fault could possibly lie with them in the search for new life. Still she kept noticing how the longing corroded into despair and, for some unexplained reason, guilt would rise in her. It was on the feast of the Holy Innocents that she went to the funeral of an old teacher who guided her gently through the infant classes back in the city where she grew up. Sister Ann had been a teaching legend through three generations and was known for her patience and caring when strictness and severity were in style in the convent in the sixties. Paying tribute to her, the priest reminded the crowded convent chapel that Sister Ann, for all the love in her, had no children to call her own, but that she had spent her years with what he called 'the life-giving touch'. 'With her,' he said, 'there was no echo of Rachel weeping for her children, refusing to be comforted. Jesus Christ said that he had come to give life, and life to the full. Sister Ann gave her life to enhancing life for others – for the slow learner in her classroom, for the poor man who came to the soup kitchen, for the distressed mother in her office.' 'If your life has been brought to a glow because of her,' the priest went on, 'perhaps the best tribute you can pay her this day is to go out and kindle life again for those who are smouldering in the ashes of loneliness, poverty, bereavement or even hunger.'

She left the convent chapel, faced the brisk December day and felt strangely touched by life again. Some people are remembered, or live on, in their children. Others live on in their work, and others again in the quality they brought into the lives of others. An ornamental cherry tree, in a garden close to the bus stop, had one branch of buds threatening to open totally out of season. Kate knew that God worked at his creation in or out of season – and she knew she would wait for his good time, by being life and hope and joy to others in the waiting time.

The Magi

It was always this week that the people who ran the residential home began to put up the streamers and tinsel of Christmas. Old Joseph saw it as the beginning of his retreat into loneliness and isolation. The advertising jingles and the emphasis on celebration, and even the goodwill of the local carol singers, did nothing but underline the emptiness of the season without the presence of his own family. He was glad that he didn't throw out the Christmas cards from his son and daughter in 1987, for every year since, he took them out of the suitcase on top of the wardrobe, and displayed them in his own room as if they had come in with the morning post. The greetings – 'With love, Father' – and 'To a dear Daddy' had an empty hollow ring to them five Christmases later.

Old man I love you
but how can I tell you
your world is yesterday
mine is today.
We sit together not so often now
in restless silence
drinking beer
or watching football
like it used to be father
when you and I were young.
I love your callused hands
They paid across the board
for my college education.
Yet it's that same degree
that makes me a stranger
when I come to see you.

Are you surprised at the world's loss of memory
still the spirit of the old is born in their young.
The apples fall not far away from the family tree.

(Paraphrase of *Papal Bulls & English Muffins*, Joe McCarthy, Paulist
Press, 1865 Broadway, NY 10023)

If Christmas plays the birth of Christ on full organ while we run
down the lanes of childhood in search of sentiment or the values of
yesterday, and if the early darkness on Christmas evening finds us
replete and empty at the same time, maybe it's because we have left
the Josephs of this world alone in their silent day and all too silent
night. For so many old people, the only Christmas gift they want is
our presence and not our presents. But we feel so ill at ease with
silence that we want to fill it with endless clatter and talk about ourselves. When they want us to listen, we begin by giving advice or
telling them why they shouldn't feel the way they do, and we do
nothing but trample all over their feelings. Then when we fuss and
do things for them which they can quite capably do for themselves,
we do nothing but contribute to their fear. But the worst silence of
all is when we take it for granted that they know how much they
are still appreciated and that the calloused hands or arthritic fingers
are symbols to us of the love and caring poured into our lives.

If we cannot tell our love to them, then there will be no vision of
angels or heavenly choirs over the hill country beyond the window
of these islands this Christmas.

On Christmas evening, my old friend Joseph had sunk lower in his
chair from the year before – but in the afternoon three old friends
came to see him and they each brought him a present – a book
about the old Great Northern Railway, a box of American tobacco,
and a half bottle of his favourite whiskey, and for over an hour they
heard about the glory of steam and engines, and old stations. The
magi had come again, he later told me, and, as he closed the window
of his room against the night frost, he was afraid to look out on the
hills in case he heard angels sing and the other folk in the home

would dismiss the story because of the two long drawn out drinks he had, before sleep closed down another Christmas day.

Waltzing leaves

It had been the week of waltzing leaves. The hills of the Glenelly Valley were radiant with colour as the gold and red of the trees were caught in snatches of autumn sunlight. I watched a group of schoolchildren get involved in this dance of death in the playground as they scooped up handfuls of the crisp leaves and threw them to the capricious wind, which flung them into new and wild circles. For all the infectious joy of the children, I felt the loneliness of the season for I couldn't feel happy loving the colours of death. I caught a falling leaf and saw in it the story of all our lives – the story of your seasons and mine.

There is a poignant beauty in autumn, with its calm days and sense of completion, but it comes each year with its reminder of our mortality. We had our springtime, the childhood days of endless meanness when all our problems were absorbed by parents and grannies. The summer of our lives headed in new purpose, a career, life's vocation, marriage and new life, and for all its beauty it went hand in hand with suffering and pain, and then, just as the first frosts nipped the leaves so the twinges of pain and the greying hair heralded the dying season of our lives.

The Bible echoes this in the Book of Sirach:

> Like clothes every body will wear out, the age old law is, Everybody must die.

And while these thoughts drifted through my mind like the tumbling leaves, I remembered that I had grasped a brown, life-drained leaf that year in the month of June. A tree had been stripped of its bark by a runaway tractor and its winter gripped it in full growth. The tree of our country has just survived an accident of history and too many found the spring hope or summer glow of their lives plunged into the fall of suffering on the winter of death long before their time. Still the dead leaves are transformed by winter's rain and snow to become the rich humus for new growth. There is no wasted life in God's plan, and for all the pain and parting of our bereavements in the Province, God is working already in the unseen beauty of another season.

For all the twinge of sadness, the autumn should also ripen our thinking into the hope that we will see a new generation of people who will see no value in disrupting the natural seasons of any person's life, but who will encourage each other to enjoy the changing patterns of life and the God-given season of our days. Maybe then we too will yet come to discover the secret of the serenity of the falling leaves.

Gentle prophet

It was in the smoke-filled room of a little country pub, which gloried in the title of 'Hotel', that I found myself one winter evening for the birthday party of a remarkable man. Despite the cautious words of the family doctor at his birth, he had lived to see his thirtieth year, and his friends, who were many, had decided to express their admiration and gratitude to him in a way that didn't call for words.

I first knew him as a delicate mongol boy who hadn't the breath for games or the heart for leaving his mother to mix with the neighbours' children. Now, here he was, sporting a new suit and exploring the intricacies of the new transistor the local lads had bought for him.

We buried him on a March day when even the sun defied the grip of winter. His sister's reflection at his requiem caught his very essence:

> Joseph, you who walked to a different rhythm –
> Because you heard a different beat –
>
> The heart of one who never faltered
> Down the road of suffering.
>
> You, whose hand, like his, was eagerly outstretched to clasp in love and friendship all who passed you on the way.
>
> For you there were no young or old,
> no rich or poor,
> no king or jesting fool.

Your eyes were far too innocent to make distinctions.
Too clear from gazing through windows at sun and shadow
playing over your rainbowed hills, teasing you with glimpses of
eternity.
Too full of wonder at starlit skies and the joy of each new day.

Everybody knew him, and everyone in ten townlands, at least,
realised that, despite his obvious handicap, he had brought a certain gentleness to our lives and had forced all of us to look at ourselves a little closer. Here, in this country where geography had
made people neighbours, and history tried to make them enemies,
he saw no borders. He believed in people, worried with the families
of the sick, wept at our funerals and was saddened by the life's
blood of the Sperrins draining away in emigration. His country to
him was more about people and living than about territory and
dying. When he prayed, he didn't rely on words. He was Catholic,
Presbyterian, Anglican, Methodist and Baptist, as there was no
room in his mind for the details of doctrinal division, and when the
Salvation Army or the Brethren expressed their praise in song on
Saturday evenings in the town, he would, with obvious delight,
give rhythmic support to God.

His politics were simple too. Every man and every woman and
every child was his country, and flags were only for flying at festi-
vals. He wore a shamrock on St Patrick's Day with the same enthusiasm that sported the orange emblem in July, and at election time he
travelled the country with whichever friend gave him a lift.

The age of the prophets, we sometimes think, were those dim distant years long before Christ tramped the dusty roads of Palestine.
Isn't it strange how seldom it strikes us that God still chooses the
weak to confound the strong, in times when the strong do little
more than confuse the weak? The birthday party, I now reflect, was
the honouring of such a prophet who spoke a simple message of
love and life in the face of news bulletins about hate and death. He
whispered hope against ghettos who screamed out their denomina-

tion; and when he was misunderstood or hurt by the callous remarks of those who didn't wear their handicaps so openly, he didn't ration out his measured forgiveness. He smiled and walked away. On the night of his birthday, at least, he wasn't without honour among his own people.

The local bakery, I remember, delivered a cake towards the end of the night. It had no candles, but then, I thought, it didn't need any. When one man lived out Christ's invitation to be a light in the world so perfectly, candles lost their symbolism and meaning. Someone turned on his transistor for a football result before we left. News headlines told of heartbreak in another two homes. He picked up his present and faced the outside darkness with a smile. The prophet had yet a long way to go.

Sound of a distant sea

He was drunk beyond his means. A stubble of two weeks hadn't taken on the dignity of a beard, and his clothes served as pyjamas and his threadbare everyday wear. He spotted me in Trafalgar Square and shouted at me as I pretended not to notice: 'Hey priest, the incense has got up your nose.' I stopped and went back with anger scarcely concealed. He laughed, 'You're mad now, priest, but you were passing on the other side.' Just then Christ's story about the Good Samaritan swamped me and the pride died. We sat down among the feeding pigeons where he suggested that I might buy him a burger. He ate half of it and wrapped the rest in the container which he stuffed into his deep pocket. 'I'll keep this for Taffy, he eats nothing.'

Oblivious to the thronging tourists, he told me a long story of confusion after Dunkirk, a broken home and a creeping feeling of uselessness that led to bouts of alcohol and rough living in London. He invited me to come and see Taffy, whom we found lying in a disused doorway below Charing Cross Station. While Taffy quoted Dylan Thomas, punctuated by hiccups, his old friend removed the cold remains of the burger and pleaded with him to eat.

It was an act of perfect kindness, for I saw this homeless alcoholic working and caring for those who shared his cold and dreary world, while I, and many like me, go on thinking that charity is a respectable virtue exercised by the comfortable to the less fortunate … and do you know, we are better at giving to the anonymous poor at the other end of the world, than we are at learning from the poor on our own doorstep.

I think it was Mother Teresa who said that charity is not about giving away material things, it is about giving something of ourselves.
In his novel *You can't go home again*, Thomas Wolfe describes a drab
and dreary scene in Brooklyn one March day:

> A group of down-and-out men stand at a street corner. 'Four
> hours they stand there,' he writes, 'and they are waiting for
> nothing.' The streets are so narrow and crowded with hunger
> and there is no one there who remembers the sea.

If, on our own streets, so many wait for nothing, then a simple word
of recognition from you and me, the passers-by, might be the beginning of hope for them and freedom for ourselves. Our biggest fault
is seriousness. We take ourselves too seriously. We cosset our dignity to the exclusion of so many colourful people and personalities
who go on telling us from their vulnerability that to love is to risk
rejection, to live fully is to risk dying and to hope is to risk despair
... but risk we must because the parable of the old man in Trafalgar
Square was a lesson in taking risks. As I sat with him that day, I
became conscious that I was chained by certainties. The risk-taker
has a sense of freedom. The day I met him, I was taking a short summer course in philosophy close by. Now that I cast my mind back to
that summer, I think the old man in the Square had more answers
than I ever had.

Epiphany

There is a dearth of wise men today. Few and far between are the
peacemakers or justice brokers who come from East or West, North
or South. It's not easy either to pick out stars when our skies are
washed in the light haze of the advertiser, or when we are asked to
focus our eyes a little lower on the so-called stars of the playing
fields or popular music. Yet, on the eve of Epiphany, at small family
gatherings, wise men were introduced into our Christmas cribs to
remain there a few short days. The English poet, T. S. Eliot, wrote
about the same magi:

> A cold coming we had of it
> Just the worst time of year
> For a journey
> And such a long journey ...

This morning, in the darkness of January, we all experience the cold
coming to this place, cold in body, or perhaps colder in mind and
soul. The putting aside of winter darkness temporarily by the lights
of Christmas is over and we settle down to the cold reality of families dispersing again, of new year bills and the uncertainty of the
year ahead and what it might hold out to us in pain, parting, or
even peace. The journey through any year may have been, like that
of the Magi, undertaken in the face of setbacks, betrayal of friends
or in the loss of health. The desert of doubt could have been the
path of everyday in an age which pays attention only to the evident.
It's not easy to go on searching for the living God in the crib setting
when so many seemingly happy people declare that they can get on
quite well without him.

For many, this is the worst time of year. Psychologists keep talking about the post-Christmas depression, for the season seldom lives up to its commercial promise. We can never capture again the days when we ran down the lanes of childhood in the tinselled season of Christmas. We feel bad about the dark days of January without a hint of spring in them and there is little consolation in the crib annual reunion with shepherds and wise men. It would seem that the wise men knew what they were looking for. Two thousand years later we are not so sure. We half-believe our horoscopes, but dazzling stars are likely to be comets or man-made space stations reflecting sunlight. It's the age when imagination tends to be confined to the infant classroom.

Still, each year at this time, I call to mind the people who became the Epiphany stars for me. They never heard the roar of approval from full football terraces. They never produced a recording or became household names in theatre or cinema. They got their names in the paper only at their deaths. But they did point unerringly to Christ by the quality of their lives.

There was that old Polish man in the nursing home near Bedwelty in Wales. He came to the valleys after the war when his homeland was lost to Russia and his wife and two daughters were last seen on a train to a concentration camp. The insidious coal dust in the mines had invaded his lungs and every breath was full of pain and discomfort. His suffering, in the years I knew him, was paralleled by a terrible loneliness. For all that, every visitor to the home was drawn towards his bed because of his gentleness and humour. On his deathbed, he would tell me that Jesus was his constant companion and friend. This Jesus proved his loyalty to him down through all the years of bitter pain because he helped him drink the chalice of suffering. 'We drank it,' he said, 'sip about.' Many saw that Star from the East and came to the presence of Christ.

'Let your light shine,' said Jesus. Maybe this feast asks us to guide others to a meeting place with Christ. Otherwise we will just tolerate the Magi for another day or two, put them back in their box, and store them, and maybe Christ, safely away for another year.

On Jordan's Banks

On a late August day, I was part of a group who were on pilgrimage to the Holy Land. We had been to the shores of the Sea of Galilee and saw Cana in relative comfort that morning. In the late afternoon, the priest leader invited us to stand in the waters of the River Jordan and renew our promises of Baptism. For various reasons, about a dozen people declined the invitation and preferred to stay dryshod on the riverbank. An exasperated Munster farmer muttered all evening about 'people who wouldn't dip a toe in the water'. The Christmas season fades away. The tree has been given over to the incinerator or to the shredder, the decorations look tired and out of place. The bottles have gone to the collecting bins and we are anxious to get rid of all the evidence of the festive season. A new year, with all its resolutions, is uppermost in our minds.

The liturgy moves on too. The days of the Bethlehem stable, with its simplicity, are behind us. The wise men have taken a different road home. The shepherds are back on the cold hills and there is no music beyond the mountains nor do they see lights in the night sky. It is the time for normal living when the daily human plod takes up its rhythm again.

Jesus had no need to go down to the Jordan river along with all those who sought repentance and a new life free from the sins of the past. He had proved his unity with this human race by being born in a shepherd's cave outside Bethlehem. Perhaps it was in the gesture of going down into the river that Jesus emphasised his unity with a sin-stained humanity. Maybe that is why the early church celebrated the feast of the Incarnation. Jesus Christ, our Saviour, would not pick his steps carefully through the sordid path of human sin, but he would be there with forgiveness and endless understanding.

At our baptisms we were given a name which our parents borrowed from family history. Here in the Jordan, John calls out a name for Jesus, a name that would stay with him forever:

'Here is the Lamb of God who takes away the sins of the world.'

That is his 'baptismal name' and it has given endless hope to men and women who felt that sin had swamped them. This is the name that holds out hope to you and me, when we feel that we have failed God badly, when we wouldn't dip our feet in the cold water of today's world, where poverty, hunger or hate chills everyday life.

The season of Christmas passes. Many turn into their Christian churches throughout the world to worship at the feast of Christmas and feel the warmth of their childhood faith again. Today, Jesus would invite us into the real world of the Incarnation, where we would be the enfleshed risen Christ for those who are burdened with pain or perplexity, for those fragile with failure, and for all who are afraid to get their feet wet in helping to redeem a world which Jesus Christ loved and loves so much.

Off by heart

An old school friend, now a dairy farmer, was recalling our college days in Derry. His memories were gentle and his appreciation of his teachers was refreshing at a time when all old sores are paraded for all to see and hear. He wasn't altogether happy with one aspect of his religious classes. He was weak at the gospels, he told me, and being unable to recall a parable or miracle, he had to learn a chapter or two by heart. There and then he began chapter nine of St Mark's Gospel and continued without fault up to the eleventh verse of the Transfiguration story.

That brought me back to a night in a West End theatre in London when I went to see a one-man show by Alec McCowen. Alone on the stage, he told the gospel story of Mark without script. It was rivetting theatre, for the words of scripture took on new life. In a strange way it was probably the first time I knew the meaning of – the Word of God is alive.

That night in London will remain with me for one word, which I had read often, but never saw. It was the word 'immediately'. It gave a certain urgency to the gospel as if Mark were impatient to get home the lesson of Jesus, the suffering servant, who had put his full trust in God.

Scholars tell us that, with its narrative urge to move the story on, there is a clue that Mark wrote this gospel to be heard as a complete story, the way I heard it from that talented actor in the London theatre. It was as a pastor he presented this action-packed story. He wrote for a people torn by persecution, not for biblical analysts or theological debate. In this pacy gospel, Mark asks all of us to reflect on the person and destiny of Christ, and see our own discipleship now when the world calls for courageous witness.

Suffering is the common thread that binds us all together, and too often it drains away at our faith. The dark night of the soul can wipe away the presence of God. The vinegar and gall diet brings on the heart's drought. Mark's gospel will set about helping all of us to find sense in our own suffering and purpose in our pain. We will discover that our own pain is not due to the forgetfulness of God. We will come to know that the handicapped newborn is not the result of some divine clumsiness. We will begin to see our own pain intertwined with that of Christ in the whole drama of salvation. Instead of waiting for this breathless gospel in Sunday installments of a few verses, why not take it up some evening and read it in its entirety, and know again the compassion, urgency, and great love of Jesus Christ. Then later in the year, take it up again and read it through your pain. In that gospel you will discover the truth of Psalm 33:18:

'The Lord is close to the brokenhearted.'

The French writer, François Mauriac, says that we are hardly conscious of the cross in our youth but, he goes on:

As the body develops and grows,
the flesh becomes heavy and drags on the nails.
What a time it takes for us to realise that we are
born crucified.

My schoolfriend, worried by BSE and falling milk prices, accepted my invitation to take up the gospel again. He knew little about the cross when he first learned off the verses of Mark. Now it made more sense to him, even if the transfigurations on the Tyrone hills were few and far between.

Places apart

I think we all have sacred places in our lives. Perhaps it is their beauty which has stayed with us and calls us back – or maybe it's their history and their association with people whose lives have touched us deeply. Some places are sacred because we have made them so, by setting them aside as shrines where we hope to encounter God. Throughout our lives we are a pilgrim people, a people on the move passing through the world with its bustling busyness, sometimes tired with its empty sideshows and sometimes conned by the trickery of the commercial magic man who tries to convince us that life is without end. There are times when we trudge through the gloom of grey days of sickness, pain and parting, and it may be then that our sacred place calls us to discover beauty, eternity or that moment of elusive peace. At other times, we go to listen to the voices of yesterday and gather strength again from the memory of those who shaped us by their love and friendship.

So I go back along the winter roads to the great sycamore tree that grows in Myles' field, close to the crossroads in a mountain parish set high in the mountains of County Tyrone. It had reached its full height when I was a boy and it seemed to have been there forever, for my grandfather had his resting spot where the tree had an area of burn marks where he tapped out the burning tobacco dregs from his pipe on summer evenings at harvest time. I must have counted the coming of seven springtimes on it, before leaving home for college days in the city. The tree was the Mount Everest I had to climb. It was a stately ship in full sail when its crowning glory of green leaves caught the wind in full summer, and it was my secure refuge when childish pranks spelt trouble at home. Down the years, when life became dreary, I would go back to the tree and surround myself with memories as I ran down the lanes of childhood again – and those days were always bedecked with the wildflowers of joy. The tree is old now. This autumn, when I stopped by, it sighed with sadness in an unseasonal gale. I'm sure its remaining seasons could be counted on its great branches.

For me the tree is sacred, for it continues to have within the rings that count its years, the history of our family and that of a closeknit neighbourhood. It's easy to play laments for the springtime of our lives when all was fresh and full of promise. We see little beauty in the autumn of middle age, or the onset of our individual winters when pain and loneliness leave us vulnerable. The old sycamore keeps telling me, year after year, that all our seasons have their own blessings and beauty. Even the fallen leaves fertilise the earth for a new spring.

When I look at the tree in mid winter, it tells me in its nakedness that I too must let go of things of yesterday and surrender a bit more to God, the Lord of all our seasons.

* * *

Friends of mine in Florida made up their minds that I would like to see a museum in Gainesville during a short stay there some years ago. I don't remember much about the exhibits but was unhappy at the way I was being rushed from one section to another by a crowd which seemed intent in getting to the museum shop and the coffee bar. On the way home, at speed on the Interstate Highway 75, we lost power and had to limp off the motorway to find a garage. Fortuitously that brought me to a place that will live with me forever. I found myself in a beautiful quaint little village called Micanopy whose pace of life belonged to another century. With its old film set appearance, its second hand bookshops and woodcarving stalls, it was all under the care of unhurried men and women who had time to talk, listen or keep silent as we browsed. Somewhere beyond the trees, the incessant drone of the wheels of commerce on Highway 75 became an intrusion.

Every year of our lives is a rush. Christmas year after year is traded as the only antidote to the early darkness and depression of November. So the carols of the season came to us soon after Halloween. We are being whisked through life like tourists through any city. We must only see the glitter and the man-made temples, but we can not tarry to savour the character or the history of the place. We are piloted at speed now from Halloween to Christmas, to Mother's day, to Easter, to holiday time and back to autumn again, and we might be missing life itself.

There are children growing up who have never seen the arrival of the swallows, the departure of the wild geese, or even a sunset over the ocean. I heard of a taxi driver who prided himself on getting an old Chinese visitor to his hotel having saved ten minutes on the cross city fare. 'And what will you do with the ten minutes?' came the polite question in return. There is a little phrase which keeps coming up in the Bible: 'at the appointed time.' Great moments were in God's good time, but we go on being impatient for tomorrow, next week, next year. The Sanskrit wisely reminds us:

> Look to this day, for yesterday is but a dream and tomorrow is only a vision, but today well lived makes every yesterday a dream of happiness and every tomorrow a vision of hope.

In Micanopy, with its endless reminders to savour the present moment, I bought a piece of native craft work. On it were appropriate words from American writers Stair and Lucas: 'If I had my life to live over, I would be sillier than I have been this trip ... I would have moments, just moments one after another, instead of living years ahead of each day ... I would pick more daisies.'

We got the car fixed and got back to the Interstate Highway again. According to an electronic clock on a billboard it was 89°F, 18.32 hours, and there were only 47 days to Christmas.

* * *

Not far from Dublin, near the town of Navan, is the headquarters of the Columban Fathers at a place called Dalgan Park. Founded in 1916 by two Irish priests, this new missionary group was assigned to Hanyang in China in 1920 and there they remained until expelled by communists in 1952. Since that small beginning, its priests have gone across the world – to Burma, Korea, Japan, the Philippines and South America.

At the back of the chapel in Dalgan Park, there are over twenty photographs of priests who died violently in the course of their ministry, from remote river valleys of China to Montego Bay in Jamaica. The place, however, which calls out to me is a new wing of the building for the old, retired and sick missionaries whose wandering for Christ is now confined to the corridors and the garden walks in the gentle setting of County Meath.

There are men there whom I read about in their missionary magazine forty years ago. To a young boy, there was something heroic about men like Philip Crosbie of Australia and Thomas Quinlan who survived the three winter death march in the Korean War. Priests like James Doody, Patrick Usher, James Devine and James McGonigle, who worked tirelessly and suffered in the Kachin Hills of Burma during the war, seemed very tall beside the local priest in our mountain parish, who lived an unhurried rural life where pastoral challenges were few. In the snug setting of our winter fireside I read about Luke O'Reilly and Patrick Reilly who survived the bitter confinement of Chinese jails, and there was Patrick Howe who reluctantly had to leave the Kachin people in Burma after a lifetime of ministry there.

The wards and the rooms in that sick bay are quiet. The occasional call for help, the half suppressed moan, breaks the silence now and again. The river paths of the Yangtse are far away now, the green jungle of Burma is a confused memory, and the words of the Kachin dialect are intermingled with their whispering prayer. Their lives of wandering for Christ as missionaries are coming to an end. And when they sit in their chairs or share a summer seat, I wonder if they hear the musical laughter of children down a village street at dusk, or hear the great bell of the temple, or do they see beyond the windows the white herons on the river bank near a distant mission station or the thick forests near Kwang-Ju. Now and again, when the smile returns, I think that beyond the rosebeds they sniff the jasmine again. Theirs was a long journey from eager mission days when they left Tilbury docks to preach the gospel in the Far East until these days when sickness has bowed them or the burden of years has broken them a bit.

Near the main road to Dublin, Columban missionaries with the two founders are laid to rest in a simple cemetery. Their gravestones say little – a name, a date of ordination and the day of death – but God knows the full story.

* * *

Nothing much passed on the road beyond the big window of our primary school in the quiet mountain parish of home in Co Tyrone. There was the occasional horse and cart, the spluttering tractor or the doctor's car. Then one afternoon we abandoned the desks completely and watched mesmerised as trucks, jeeps and troop carriers roared their way to mountain military manoeuvres. The troops from America had come to us on their way to war in Europe. That evening, standing tall on sentry duty at our parish hall, I saw, for the first time, a man who was black. He gave me chewing gum and two bars of chocolate. His name, he said, was 'Chalky White'. Days later, the parish was quiet again. Chalky and the rest had gone to Europe. Years later, almost by chance, I met a man in Florida who had been in Northern Ireland with the American forces. He checked out some old records and found that Chalky had died on the beach at Normandy. In a special way now, the war cemeteries of Normandy are sacred stops in this search for places which call out to me.

When I go there now, I look out to sea at Arrowmanches late in the evening and try to visualise the mayhem, the tragedy and the courage of that June day in 1944 when over a hundred thousand fell to gain a foothold in Europe. Then I drive to the cemeteries and walk through the tombs and look at the inscriptions as short as the lives they mark. The date June 6th keeps repeating on stone after stone. Over at the American cemetery at San Laurent-Sur-Mer, with its endless rows of neat crosses, set in manicured lawns, there are few names recorded but I walk through the paths and know that 'Chalky' is out there somewhere.

When I finally leave the war cemeteries, I feel challenged by the young men who rest in the gentle earth of France far away from Atlanta, Philadelphia, Aberdeen or the Rhonda Valley. They all had their dreams. They were unique individuals who had come to France that summer day, not as tourists to a welcoming beach, but as young men who had carried the prayers and hopes, the pain and the parting of those who remained at home, unsure of what was happening. But they plummeted to explosive death and suddenly, as the poet Brooke put it:

> There was a corner of a foreign field that was forever set aside as that of another nation.

The tides ebb and flow on the beaches of Normandy. That dreadful June day has only a few relics left there, while across the world and here many have just fading memories of those who went to France on the morning tide and never came back.

Every time I look out over the endless graves, I know in my heart that war is an obscenity. The cross tells me that since the death of Jesus Christ, there is no need for any human being to spill the blood of another, either on the sands of France or in the familiar streets of Northern Ireland. And every June 6th, I think of 'Chalky' White and pledge myself to peace once again.

* * *

Despite the tension and the constant threat of violence in the Middle East, many people still see that region as the Holy Land, with the places associated with Jesus Christ held sacred, while Moslems hold dear the Dome of the Rock. With a group of pilgrims, I made my guided way in the oppressive heat of a late August weekend. I pushed my way along the Via Dolorosa, visited the church of the sepulchre, the Kedron Valley and many other places on the guide's long list. For some reason, nothing held my attention or interest until we went to Bethlehem and I left the group and made my way to the Shepherd's field. This was the hill country where Jesus was born and it was unspoilt by buildings and, as I looked at the mountain caves, it struck me that Christ could have been born in any one of them. The marked holy places were lost underneath ornate churches or basilicas, but this was untouched and I felt that I was looking at the hill profiles which rose before Mary and Joseph on that nervous night of full inns.

As I sat there, my mind filled with a mixture of nostalgia and peace, the quiet calm of the Shepherd's field was shattered by the high scream of a fighter jet, climbing steeply into a clear blue sky. That place of peace invaded by the harsh sound of war has remained with me ever since.

Wasn't it above the hills that the angels sang their welcome to the newborn Jesus and included all folk of goodwill? Over the hills to the east, war was simmering, unholy war in the holy land, while back to the west was my homeland, where almost two thousand years later, war was wasting men, women and children on the familiar streets and lanes of Ireland. At that time, I remember a public crib destroyed in a crude bombing of a town hall. Wasn't it the poet Hardy who pointed the accusing finger when he wrote:

'Peace upon earth' 'twas said
We sing and pay a million priests to bring it
After two thousand years of Mass,
We've got as far as poisoned gas.

At the time of year when we get caught up in the decorations of Christmas, and when many try to cram the year's deficit of goodwill into a few presents, I can no longer look at the crib without the reminder of the war plane over the hills of Bethlehem. It somehow reminds me that Christmas is not a hero, not a stockpiling of arms. Christmas is a child inviting all of us to be so defenceless, so dependent on each other that we no longer attack, no longer dwell on our differences, no longer march down the roads which lead to war. Saviour is the oldest name for Jesus and Saviour means healing, rescuing and reconciling. The law of the strongest holds no sway in the stall of the Christmas crib. We could forget about the challenge of

Christmas if it becomes only a winter festival to distract us momentarily from the gathering darkness of these days.

The shepherd's field will stay with me, but the carols of Christmas
and the bells of midnight will always be drowned a little by the
scream of the climbing jet.

* * *

Setting out again on pilgrimage to places which are sacred to me, I
find myself drawn again to a small clearing in the forest of the
Gortin Glens in Northern Ireland. It was there one midsummer day
that I suddenly found myself swamped by silence. When I arrived
at the spot, there was a slight rustle of a summer breeze astir in the
woods. Then, high above, a jet with its vapour trail was leaving
Europe behind as it nosed westwards out over the Atlantic, an
occasional bird chirped, while, far away in the fields below, a distant tractor laboured through its gears. Then, quite suddenly, the
breeze died, the birds held their song, the jet was beyond the coast.
A total blessed silence had come down. I don't know how long it
lasted, but in that moment I suddenly felt totally alone on the planet
earth and knew the presence of God, a God who was content with
the beauty and the order of the earth and the heavens. I was afraid
to move in case a rheumatic joint would creak in protest, so I sat
motionless, even tuning my ear to take in more of the silence. In a
moment this oasis of peace linked up with the lesser moments of
silence in my life – the hospital ward in Belfast the night my father
died, the early vigil of prayer in the darkness of a Cistercian
Monastery, and the inner silence that almost drugged my mind the
night an old friend ended his life without a word of explanation or
apology. And I thought of the remarkable author-monk, Thomas
Merton, who wanted to move away from the silence of the
monastery at Gethsemani in Kentucky to seek a quieter hermitage
because, as he wrote:

'the cloister is as crowded as a Paris street.'

And when he found the hermitage in the woods not far from the monastery, the silent place became the springboard for a fresh new adventure, as he turned himself outwards to the world of pollution, nuclear arms and the hanging clouds of war.

That day on the hills above Gortin, I think I discovered a rare gift from God which came in the silence when all the world seemed to have gone away. It was the gift of wonder, and I felt at one with the Rabbi Heschel who wrote in the preface to a book of Yiddish poems:

'Lord I did not ask for success,
I asked for wonder and you gave it to me.'

The moment passed. Another jet droned away to the west. A helicopter kept an eye on the strifetorn land below and the wind freshened. The Mount Tabor experience of transfiguration was gone and I had to come down the mountain and confront the daily din of the world's pain.

I went back there a year later. Low rain clouds scudded before a gathering wind, while here in Northern Ireland we went on experiencing the agony of half hope in the endless quest for peace.

* * *

I have been revisiting the places, the sacred spots or pilgrim places, the places apart which punctuate all our lives. I find myself at the end of the journey on the Foyle Bridge in Derry, which spans the river in architectural majesty a mile or two before it empties itself into Lough Foyle and the North Atlantic. I like to stand on the bridge when it is windswept on a late autumn or winter evening, and look down into the deep troubled waters of the river. It is a powerful parable, a lesson about life and eternity.

I knew these waters when we both were young, far away upstream in County Tyrone. I remember the endless days of summer that seem to mark all our memories, and the river was just a dancing little trout stream which surrendered the occasional brown trout to the short-trousered boy who added ounces to its weight with each telling. But we both grew older and filled up with our own importance – the river even changed its name twice as it made takeover bids for lesser tributaries and its pace changed. The laughing days of tumbling streams were a long way back. I too had taken on a lot of life's baggage. There was no time for the patient wait with fishing rod. Fish could be got instantly on supermarket slabs and the weighing scales told no lies. And now it had come to this. The waters below are old now. There were days of joy surely. The Foyle is celebrated in song, and the melody caught on violin or flute in some far flung place of exile brought back youth and friends and days of untroubled peace. But, here below the bridge, that is coming to an end. The river still fights for its name, history and identity, even as the tide waters threaten to steal it away into the eternity of the ocean, while I ponder the words of the Irish poet Yeats:

Though leaves are many, the rest is one
Through all the lying days of my youth
I swayed my leaves and flowers in the sun
Now I may wither into truth.

If I stand on the other side of the bridge, I can look upstream to the south beyond the lights of the city of Derry and the memories of childhood days flow back with the river. All the great Christian writers tell us that we should be homesick for heaven, that we should count off the days in our twilight years like I did on the cubicle calendar when I was at boarding school, waiting for Christmas. But I am like the river, reluctant to let go even though I know that, like the Foyle's dark waters, there is no going back. Maybe it's all a tribute to God who made the earth so beautiful that we are loathe to part. But sometimes, on a high summer day, from the Foyle Bridge I can sniff the ocean to the north, and its charm and immensity call me, and somedays I know that only an eternity with God will make sense of all our journeying.

Pieta, you are not marble –
we are

Easter was late in nineteen-eighty-four, and first communion day in early May saw the little County Tyrone village church still bedecked with the Easter blooms and the Alleluia banners of paschal joy. That morning there was no containing the joy as girls, resplendent in gowns and veils, came down the aisle and out into the early summer sun. Families intermingled, teachers were thanked and a hundred cameras froze the moment for album history. It was then that I noticed her, sitting alone in the church quietly at home with her thoughts. She moved to a side altar and knelt in prayer before a statue of Michelangelo's Pieta, that marvellous expression of compassion where Mary holds the dead Christ on her knee. Then she reached into her handbag for the tissue that would absorb the tears that threatened her gentle make up. The laughter and conversation from the churchyard didn't distract her as she quietly composed herself and went out to join in the joy of her niece's first communion day. It was later in the day that I remembered a biting March day, seven years before, when her husband and oldest son stood wrapped in grief with me as I prayed over the little white coffin of her week-old child, Emma. That May morning would have been Emma's first communion day and, even though Emma was in closer communion with God, she mourned her white veiled absence.

The following morning, I stood before the Pieta in the church and felt guilty about the lack of sensitivity in me that made me think that grieving for an infant could be confined to one or two years. As I looked at this carving of Michelangelo's, where Mary holds the dead Christ on her knee, I saw its universal meaning. It articulates in expressive marble, a high moment of human grief; a perfect mother grieving over a perfect son, innocence sacrificed, punishment without fault. Mary's grief was compassion. It was a grief endured for others. Holding Jesus, her son, I saw her hold the pain of the world and I remembered an old prayer fr⌐ ⌐ an American bishop, who too felt guilty about his own lack of sensitivity in the face of another sorrow. 'Pieta', he wrote, 'Pieta, you are not marble – we are.'

Over the next few days, as the summer began to touch the earth and the frosts of winter finally let go their grip, I couldn't get the memory of a mother's quiet grief out of my mind. Why did God let this mother carry her child to life and then take it away before she had time to greet and welcome the infant to this earth? How could a good God steal away this sleeping child? Does a loving God allow a boy or girl, who never walked a step or mouthed one syllable of language, to suffer pain with not a word to tell us where it hurt? We can understand pain in the parent. We can cope with suffering in the sinful earth, we can absorb somehow the aching famine in grown people, but we can't watch the wide-eyed child with begging bowl and the troublesome flies in famine wasted lands. We will raise flags and sing anthems over coffined soldiers, victims of the atrocity of war – but a God who loved children – why? Why?

> O God
> why did you not take her long ago
> before she died and won our minds and hearts
> and with her gentle smile and patient eyes
> entwined her life and love with ours,
> became a very part of us, a limb, an eye?
> Her long weak slender arms possessed a power
> to capture and hold us. And even ill,
> and even dead, she won't let go.
> And even though they've covered up the grave
> with stones and thorns lest jackals rave and rage,
> through shroud and stones, through wood and thorns
> she stretches out to hold me. A part of her is here,
> a part of me is there.

O God,
why did you not take her long ago
before she'd won our minds and heart?
Or is she truly yet with me? ... and I with her?
(Cothrai Gogan, *Collected Poems*)

Is part of me with her? Is part of her with me?

Somehow the human mind is at a loss for an answer that would make sense of the suffering and give purpose to the pain. One summer I walked through the old cemetery at St Augustine in Florida, where the first Christian mission to North America was established. There were tombstones, leaning with age, to missionaries and exiles but what caught all my attention were the tidy little graves for children, born a hundred years ago and who knew this life for one or two short days. I fingered the name in the worn chiselled stone of one small monument, and even then distraught parents asked God for meaning in Psalm 142:

Lord listen to my prayer
turn your ear to my appeal
you are faithful, you are just, give answer ...
I remember the days that are past
I ponder all your works
I muse on what your hand has wrought
and to you I stretch out my hands.
Like a parched land my soul thirsts for you ...
For your name's sake, Lord, save my life;
in your justice save my soul from distress.

The Lord gives, the Lord takes away

Every life is his gift, but it's only on loan for we are not permanent residents of this earth. Every person's death diminishes us, said the Poet Donne, and every birth, I believe, enriches us even if that life lasted hours instead of years. But the human mind calls to God in every generation for understanding. God be in my head and in my understanding, we pray, otherwise we can see no patterns in life, no meaning in death, no point in pain or parting.

Do not despise her centimetre size
or cut-out carton coffin
Remove your ugly boot
and measure not in ugly feet.

Do not despise her centimetre size
for angels sing and praise
around this tiny head;
and in such tiny hands, so tiny heart
salvation for the world was laid.
(Cothrai Gogan, *Collected Poems*)

Will the passing years, we wonder, ease the pain, will God ever fill
the gap between family and the dead child? Might this little mite be
forgotten as we fill our lives with plans and programmes for the
others who now demand attention in their growing years? Will that
one photograph, which captured a brief moment of life, fade
because it can't be updated in any family album? Will his or her
name be forgotten because it is not shouted at play or written with
the long spidery lines of the infant classrooms? I think not. This
child caught all our attention for its brief span. In life, the infant
would have changed our outlook and our priorities. In death, the
child will do the same and will unearth gifts for others that may lie
dormant, only pain released them. God will not fill the gap between
the parent and the dead child, for then the child would be truly
overlooked and forgotten. Dietrich Bonhoeffer, who was to die in a
world war prison camp, was painfully aware of separation.

Nothing can fill the gap when we are away
from those we love, and it would be wrong
to try and find anything.
That sounds very hard at first,
but at the same time it is a great consolation
since leaving the gap unfilled preserves the bonds
between us.
It is nonsense to say that God fills the gap.
He does not fill the gap but keeps it empty

so that our communion with another may be kept alive,
even at the cost of pain.

It was the writer Victor Frankl who said that we cannot judge a
biography by its length, we must it judge by the richness of the con-
tents, and he added: 'sometimes the "unfinished" are among the
most beautiful symphonies'. The life of every child is beautiful even
if its short existence is wrapped in so much pain for parents, brothers and sisters. Jesus never denied that tragedy was tragedy. The
death of the innocents around the time of his birth must have been a
family nightmare for his parents and later for himself, as he must
have wondered how much he was to blame. There was the loss of
his friend Lazarus for whom he wept, and he could have seen nothing in the approach to Calvary but the grief it was causing to those
who loved and followed him.

It will have to be that within his unfailing love we will find the
answer and recognise our broken hearts at home with his. Parents,
for all their faith, are human and hurt for years, but we can't forget
that a mother gave life. For nine months her body, in its discomfort
and pain, shaped the flesh and blood of a new life. Her love paced a
new heart beat. Her hope supported the delicate life womb curled
within her. She fashioned a human life – she brought to life a mas-
terpiece of individuality. For such a short span of life, as we know
it, the world was richer in joy and hope and admiration. The passing years are necessary to take the edge off human pain, to calm our
anger with God, the master of life, to take time to say farewell. Only
then might we dare to offer our praise again to the living God.

These words are from St John Chrysostom, an early Christian saint,
to a distraught father 1500 years ago:

> You have not lost your son, but have sent him on to a more gen-
> tle place. Do not say I can no longer be called 'father', for why
> would you say this when your son is still alive? Surely you did
> not part with your child, nor lose your son. Rather you were part
> of his creation and have him now in greater safety. No longer,

then, shall you be called 'father' on earth, but also in heaven. You have not lost the title father but gained it with a richer meaning.

Jesus Christ had to carry out his complete mission on earth within the brief span of three years. Yet never once do we find him in a hurry. He had time for the demanding blind beggar whose annoying cries prompted bystanders to keep him quiet. He had time for a word of consolation to the woman who touched the hem of his garment and was healed, and, even on the painful way to his execution place on Calvary, he made time to salute the courage of the women of Jerusalem. And he had time for children. He saw in them the simplicity, truth and honesty that should be the measure of all who become his disciples. He saw also in them the capacity for wonder and open-eyed joy in discovery.

Mark, in his gospel, captured the moment:

> People were bringing little children to him, for him to touch them. The disciples scolded them, but when Jesus saw this he was indignant and said to them, 'Let little children come to me; do not stop them; for it is to such as these that the kingdom of God belongs. In truth I tell you, anyone who does not welcome the kingdom of God like a little child will never enter it.' Then he embraced them, laid his hands on them and gave them his blessing.

(Mk 10:13-16, JB)

One day it will slowly dawn on us that the child we loved and lost went to God unhindered. Tears were meant for tired eyes like yours and mine. The passing years will find the other children grow into adolescence and then grow away from home. The ties to home are broken as parents watch their children say goodbye and leave to find families of their own. Some will go into exile and leave the land of birth, only to return to find us trapped in what they think is a time lag. We may understand them only with difficulty. They may not understand us at all. All the time, one child, who never knew the heat of the sun or the cold kiss of winter, is forever young, while, as one Irish poet, Sheridan, put it, we go on reaping a little of death's harvest every day. This child, with God, may still be the one who binds the past to the present, who binds the gentle earth of home to the distant place of exile. For the child never died, never aged. Life was changed, not taken away.

He will always be young.
The baffled tears will never trace a line upon his brow.
And nothing of life's littleness can bow that proud and lovely head.
No hopes, no fears can touch these sleeping eyes and sleeping ears, or teach with long and bitter lesson how the heart breaks.
Nothing can vex him now.
He is beyond the sacrilege of tears.
He will be, as he fell asleep;
(For all is left, though all is taken away)
Forever beautiful, forever young, whilst we, growing old, and lustreless, will reap a little of death's harvest every day.
… Listening for songs the heart was to have sung.

(John D. Sheridan, *Joe's no saint*, Talbot Press)

When I look again at the Pieta, I look on Mary of Nazareth and see in her a source of comfort and motherly care for this planet and its people. I see in Mary a model for endurance. On that Judean hillside, as she cradled the dead child of her womb, did she glimpse the future? When an adult dies we bury the past. When a child dies we bury the future and all those might-have-beens.

When Mary agreed to become the mother of a divine child, she took a frightening risk, but, for all the pain of Calvary she would have changed none of it. Even today, as I look at the Pieta, I think of the parents of this land who took the risk of parenthood and were pained by the loss of children – and for all that, would have changed nothing. The earth, they know, is richer for having heard one cry of their child, is richer for having been trodden on by little feet, is happier for having heard that laughter, now gone silent. The earth is holier for their brief presence.

PIETA, YOU ARE NOT MARBLE – WE ARE

With the coming of Good Friday every year, some think that the events of that day may feel removed from life. We might be able to convince ourselves that we live in less barbarous times when public executions are a thing of the past. The Christ carved in perfect proportion may now hang on a cross of silver and gold, and that can distance us from the tragedy of the Judean hillside. Parents who have lost a child, mothers who sat at the foot of the cross supporting the lifeless child of their wombs, know that the cross is not so much old and rugged, but new and with edges that eat into frail shoulders. Calvary is closer than we think. I hope none of the sympathisers on that first Calvary told Mary that there wouldn't be a word about it in twenty years. I hope that we, centuries later, will stop and see the cross on those who suffer loss this day, and never think that time has taken all the edges of suffering away.

Yet, as a Christian people, we know that death is not the end, only a change of life, and that the darkness of this day gives way to the light of Easter, that hate will give way to harmony, that separation will be forgotten in the embrace of meeting again. Having looked again this morning at the Michelangelo sculpture of Mary and her dead child, and forgetting momentarily about Easter Sunday, I will say again,

'Pieta, you are not marble, we are.'

Rebecca

His last few hours
wrapped in the drone of beaded prayer
found his drained wife
giving to the end.
Seeming to know his point of thirst
she held the sponge of water to his parched lips
… the lips she first kissed
in a breathless moment of shyness
in the hayfield on the side of Mullaghcarn mountain.
Within a towering powerful frame
he hid for sixty years.
Now, with death not the length of a litany away
a sound, half heard, struggled for understanding
in his dry throat.
She put her ear close and caught the drowning word
'Rebecca … Rebecca'.
Rebecca, the name they gave their first born
who died after two anxious hours
of delicate struggle.
Not till now
had he mentioned
her name.

Convent twilight

She sat alone in the convent chapel. The stroke had robbed her of a once powerful independence and limited life to the wheelchair and the bed. There was a day when she made her final profession in the same sanctuary. More than thirty nuns mingled with family and friends and the incense hung heavy in the air. Now the convent was in its last days. A national supermarket chain had bought the place and even her long dead sisters were to be exhumed and re-buried in the town cemetery to make way for a wine store. The evening sun caught the stained glass window and threw colours through her silver hair. She was alone with her confused thoughts.

The Irish town which lay below the windows had known her for over fifty years. She knew the heartbreak of poverty, for in her early teaching days she and her sisters had given breakfast to palefaced children who arrived shivering in the days long before buses. She watched later the scourge of emigration which bled the town of its youth and, as her pupils grew into marriage and family, she supported them in her prayer through the joys as well as through the pain of alcoholism, childlessness, violence, sickness and death. The changing church had unnerved her as old certainties gave way to breathless change and, at times, God seemed to be distant as a new generation of women found no purpose in a prayer life within the convent walls. In a few weeks time, the convent would be nothing but a building site. The old sister would move to the invalid wing of the order house thirty miles away and, hopefully, her confused mind might blur the memories and ease the parting pain.

I left the old sister alone with her God. For all those years she had been the human touch of God in an Irish town. I came out onto the street where huge advertising boards promised the town a bright, warmer and healthier future. Maybe, I began to think, the old sister's prayer and life of love would be a firmer foundation for that hope.

Marching towards Emmaus ... again

I remember a late February evening when a neighbour, passing the field where a few of us were playing football after school, told me that my father was home from hospital after a stay of four nervous weeks. The match was forgotten. The score no longer mattered. My brother and I picked up our coats and, trailing schoolbags, ran breathlessly all the way home. It was one of those memorable moments of childhood joy. The winter days of loneliness, the pain of his parting by ambulance, the reports from the hospital of his serious condition, were all things of the past. He was home, pale and with his breathing a little laboured, but spring was in the air and we ran around the country parish well into the night, letting everyone know our good news. The memory of that night comes to mind when I look again at the gospel account of the resurrection of Christ in the dying days of Lent.

Easter Sunday is all about running feet. There is the breathless Mary Magdalene racing back to tell the apostles that Jesus was no longer in the tomb. The younger John outruns the older fisherman, Peter, to see for himself if the story could be true. The disciples in Emmaus leave the unfinished meal and come with haste through the night to share their good news and boundless joy.

In the Ireland of today, so many years later, can we dare to hope, dare let ourselves look to better days, dare shout with joy, or will Easter be a day for muted alleluias, a day when we would ask Christ for a greater miracle than resurrection? We wish for a peace dropping down like a spring morning dew, a peace that would cost all of us nothing, no loss of face, no retreat from our denominational bunkers, no surrender at all. Our country, for over twenty-five years, has the uncomfortable legacy of endless bereavements, Calvarys of painful memories and ashes to make a mountain. There are many neighbours of mine in Northern Ireland who find it hard to believe in a risen Saviour when so many, who claim to be his followers, can't believe sufficiently in each other.

But, maybe, the endless Good Friday is our own fault. Maybe we are beginning to think that the cross is an integral part of the image of Northern Ireland. Since the death of Christ on the hillside all those years ago, there has been no need for any man to spill the blood of a brother in the name of God, but the sacreligious blood of too many has poured down urban gutters, or ran diluted into road margins because someone felt that their version of God had to be defended. Wouldn't we all love a little paragraph inserted into the gospel story, just before the passion narrative, telling us that all the characters are fictional and bear no resemblance to any person, living or dead? We could go on then, comfortable in the thought that it was a regrettable piece of legend, and thank God that we had no hand or part in it … But the way of the Cross still runs through our cities, along border roads, while too many of us close our eyes to the ongoing funeral processions and lower our blinds to passing death.

On Easter Sunday we learn again that truth could be put in a grave but couldn't be kept there. Jesus Christ could not be found among the dead on Easter Sunday, nor will he be found buried or entombed on any Easter Day. Why do we go on looking for him in the 'them' and 'us' mentality, when he would want us to unburden our children of the legacy of distrust and build a museum for outworn ideas and meaningless cliches? Why do we search out the dates of the dead and make them further causes of suffering when Jesus would want us to look into a new century? We set up parade commissions to keep an eye on us as we go on marching into the future backwards, as we hoist our banners and beat our drums going down the road to Emmaus.

Maybe, our Easter will finally dawn when we discover how pitifully small our differences are, when we hold them up to the searing suffering of endless refugee lines seeking a homeland of an acre or two where a tent could be tied and children could eat a frugal fistfull of food.

Easter is the celebration of that hope. The same Jesus Christ who conquered death can conquer our reluctance, if only we offer him that chance. Because of Christ there is reason for hope in new beginnings. He shared our life and our death because he became a tragic figure in a world where tragedy is commonplace. Without him, the strong could make this earth their paradise while the weak would call it hell, and the grave would be the only ambition for aimless generations.

Could we put aside the drums, rest our slogans, fold our flags and shout out our alleluias, firm and full-throated, because we have rooted our hope in this risen Easter Christ, who will fix the things that are broken and gather the scattered? He will hush the strident cries of the ghettoes which still scream out their denominations at us.

The cycle of life returns. The trees, which feigned death in the northern winter, are coming to life again and, as we listen, a single note of hope can be heard beyond the silent tragedy of Good Friday. It will expand into a marvellous chord of music which will tell us what we have always known ... that Jesus went away from us in human death to pull out the stops for glory.

Lord, you are hard
on mothers

Peggy was weary as she eased herself carefully out of the neighbour's car which had just brought her home from hospital. With her was her third son Stephen, just a week old. There had been the usual complications before he was born, but she had come to expect that, as doctors were understandably anxious about a woman who already had two physically handicapped children. She was weary but happy because Stephen was, in the words of the doctor, 'a perfectly normal child'. 'I had made up my mind to call him Stephen,' she said, 'because I felt he too would have the same useless limbs as his brothers and the name of a martyr seemed appropriate.'

As she went upstairs to put her child in the prepared cot, I began to think that we thought of martyrs in Ireland only in the context of those who died defending their God or their country. The history of this country has been punctuated by men and women who died because they felt that God needed their constant witness to the point of death, while others went to early graves because the country needed them, they felt, in the darker moments of its history. The church honoured its martyrs in ceremony and liturgical red. The country honoured its martyrs in patriotic songs and colours appropriate to the location of the cemetery, while all the time we have overlooked the white martyrdom that goes on every day in the lives of so many mothers.

Peggy, the pale young mother who came down the stairs to sink back into a chair and sip the tea with both hands clutching the cup, was such a martyr herself. Her young life had slipped away in the constant demands of two sons who had to be carried long after her strength could meet that challenge. Her life was a weekly round of home and hospital, clinics and care centres, and all the time the pain of her sons' uncertain future drained the colour from her cheeks and etched out lines of worry prematurely on her young brow.

It's not the suffering but the cause which makes the martyr, and this young mother was prepared to stand any suffering, put up with any pain, endure any inconvenience, for the love of those two boys who could only drag themselves around the street supported by uncertain crutches, which are not the usual toys of childhood.

The photograph on the bookshelf, taken in the late sixties when she was still at school, showed her laughing, bright and young, seated in the centre of the netball team. Now she sat opposite and I could see that she had put a lifetime into the years between, and the pain of it had bowed her head and stolen her youth. 'Lord you are hard on mothers,' one Irish writer has put it, 'they suffer in our coming and in our going.' When those dedicated to great causes want lessons on endurance, they need look no further than the neighbourhood door which closes on the quiet courage of those women who shape the future of a country in their care for its growing citizens. It's in her that the words of Christ, about dying so that others can have life, are most tangible.

She left me to the door as Stephen began to cry. 'He'll be walking in a years time,' she told me, 'and the sight of a child of mine doing that will be the greatest joy of my life.' I left her front door and walked down the street, wondering to myself what we owed the pale mother-martyrs who have given life and living to a country which still is quicker to remember and honour its dead.

Solemn silence

She looked out the kitchen window at the emerging beauty of the cherry tree, but couldn't enter fully into the joy of her daughter's wedding later in the day. She had seen and felt her growing excitement for weeks now and she liked her future son-in-law for his gentleness and courtesy. But the fears rose before her like the shadows cast by the dark clouds of early morning over the Tyrone hillside. She remembered her own wedding day, in the heart of January in a cold church with a minimum of liturgy, and with few of the trappings that seemed to be a necessary part of today's ritual. A short honeymoon in Dublin that was crippled with homesickness was soon forgotten in the hectic spring days on the farm and in nights of tending her ailing mother-in-law. The children came in a pattern – a girl, a boy, a girl, a boy until she gave birth to her sixth and last. The husband was a quiet man. He could never have been accused of drunkenness, neglect of his family or any element of cruelty, but there was little conversation beyond finance, local deaths, and the occasional newspaper headline. She had never eaten out with him since the day he had taken her to the Belfast hospital where there were complications with the pregnancy of her first born, who now stood at the threshold of her own marriage. There were times when she wanted to drive away in the middle of the night and leave the grey grim day-to-day existence that cried out for colour and music and dance.

On the anniversary of her wedding, which wasn't marked by any word or card, she would read again the words of her wedding ceremony. She had a small card in the Sunday missal. It had a sentence from the priest on that day, when he said that a cord of three

strands was not easily parted, and he suggested that prayer might
be that bond. It must have been the prayer that let her transcend the
greyness of the days which brought her to this day of beauty and
joy. She knew that her husband was full of pride but empty with the
thought of the oldest daughter leaving home. But why wouldn't he
give a word of praise? Why would his masculine vow of silence not
just find a dispensation on this day tinged with sadness?

Her daughter burst into the kitchen wrapped in a dressing gown,
'Look what daddy gave me,' she said, holding a triple folded cheque
for a thousand pounds! She reached for her daughter's hand and
blinked back a tear: 'God love him,' was all she could say, 'God love
him anyway.'

Carved in marble

Joe has seen six summers in the Nazareth House. The room he shared with an old neighbour, who was now deaf, looked out over the river which made its way lazily to the sea in its last few miles. The place had its comforts. It was warm, the food was good, the television gave entertainment now and again, and the grounds were seasonally beautiful, yet there was an empty corner in his life that used to haunt him in hours of loneliness. Indeed the sister in charge had noticed the cloud that overshadowed his normal brightness and good humour, and they all knew that he was the first to the post basket in the morning to find the letters that eluded him. At Christmas, the dozen cards he got never made up for the one that didn't come, and the festive celebration of the day lacked one essential memory.

His mind used go back often to the small stony farm where he grew up. He brought his young wife home to the same thatched one-storey house on an April day when American troops were camped on the river bank before the war on the beaches of Normandy. The years since had robbed him of her presence in death when she was in her fifties. One son stayed on the ungenerous land and the girls married and left – except for the youngest. He had loved her for she had a spirit of courage and daring that he never had himself, and there was adventure in her from the day she first went to school. Then one day, she told him of her plans to marry a young Presbyterian farmer. That day he pulled down the shutters, and to protect his frayed feelings he put her out of the house, ignored her letters, and went to the turf on the day of her wedding. As far as he ever thought of her, she was dead.

In the mellow days of his first brokenness, he searched out for her but the earlier hurts had made them strangers to each other. He had written every Christmas but there had been no reply. St Thomas More once wrote:

> The good that people do to us we write in sand,
> the hurt they do we carve in marble.

The sadness of his last days would be the cold marble of unforgiveness that would deny the embrace of love – and deep down he knew he was at fault. His fervent prayer had become that of a faded Hollywood actress:

> Father forgive us for not forgiving.
> Treat us tomorrow as we treat each other today.

The pity was that he hadn't said it years before.

The rest is silence

My earliest memory of prayer was the nightly rearrangement of the kitchen chairs to face the faded Sacred Heart picture. Kneeling there with rosary to hand, the onslaught of words began which included the rosary and an earlier version of the bidding prayers called the 'trimmins'. 'Speak Lord, for your servants are listening' had given way to: 'Listen Lord, for your servants are speaking.' Many things have changed since those days, but some things never change. For all the developments in liturgy and in fashions of prayer, we are still uncertain and uncomfortable when faced with silence. Yet silence is a necessary dimension of all liturgical activity. The General Instruction on the Roman Missal draws attention to the importance of silence in worship, and a foreword to an American edition of the Sacramentary puts it well:

> The proper use of silent prayer and reflection will help render the celebration less mechanical and impersonal and lend a more prayerful spirit to the liturgical rite ... Just as there should be no celebration without song, so too there should be no celebration without periods for silent prayer and reflection.

That same emphasis is found in the General Introduction to the Liturgy of the Hours, where silence is suggested so that those who pray the hours might receive in their hearts 'the full sound of the voice of the Holy Spirit'. There are natural moments for silence at the end of each psalm and on concluding the readings. Without silence, all liturgy can be reduced to an avalanche of words which leave no peace to ponder. We live in a culture of noise where silence is alien and, sometimes, to a younger generation it frightens and isolates. Yet we need silence to savour the wisdom of the psalms.

Only through silence can we hold on to the beauty of the word of God and its power. Under all the uttered or the muttered words lies a silence that is better.

The French composer Debussy once wrote, 'the only response to true beauty is silence'. When a parish or community has carefully planned the Sunday celebration of Eucharist with love and prayer, when music, readings and homily touch the pulse of the gathered congregation, then silence will be the time God will whisper to the heart.

Mark Searle expressed it beautifully:

> There is the silence of speechlessness,
> of being lost for words in the face of shock,
> delight or wonder:
> the strange, disorienting experience
> of groping for words that stretch and strain
> and break under the weight they cannot bear.
> The Lord is in his holy Temple:
> Let the earth keep silence before him.

David Philippart from Chicago prepared an inset for any parish in Chicago which wished to use it on moments of silence:

> Beginning on ... we are going to practise being silent at some points in the liturgy, being silent together. At first our silence will be awkward. Throats will cough, seats will creak, song sheets will rattle. But if we stick to it, our silence will deepen and lengthen ... Liturgy will become less a torrent of words and more a sacred celebration, an encounter with God that has a rhythm of song and speech and silence, a rhythm of action and rest.

In 1997, we celebrated the 1400th anniversary of the death of St Colmcille, I hope silence descended on the Columban gatherings for a few minutes so that we could grasp how much silence meant to him on Iona after a life of turbulent turmoil. He wrote:

Sometimes in a lonely cell
in the presence of my God
I stand and listen.
In the silence of my heart
I can hear his will
when I listen.
For I am but a servant
who is guided by his king
when I listen.

An old priest friend of mine wrote to me from hospital in the final
weeks of his life. In an uncertain hand, he called for forgiveness for
all the empty endless words he spoke at other death-beds. '... rela-
tives talk to much, fellow priests reminisce too much. I want this
death-bed din to cease. I cry out for a line of a psalm and the silence
to hear it.' He looked forward to heaven, especially to that description of it in the Book of the Apocalypse (8:1):

And when the Lamb opened the seventh seal
there was silence in heaven for about half an hour.

A Valley of Darkness

You didn't hear the birds
greet the dawn
or hear the slow lament
of Glenelly's quiet waters
tumble towards the ocean
on that mellow autumn morn.

> You walked a dark valley
> where pain fell like a November mist
> from the stately slopes of Sawel.

They say that heaven has no seasons,
but, every April day,
when the green leaves of spring
are flush with life and hope
in this scenic Sperrin valley
we will remember you.

> For you left us in the Springtime of your life.
> Now we go on withering into autumned age
> hoping that you will be waiting
> on the doorstep of eternity
> to show us around
> your heaven of peace.

The calm before the storm

When I look back at summer days in the late fifties, I think of hours of fishing and boating on Lough Erne in Co Fermanagh. One Sunday has always remained with me for its marvellous element of surprise. It was a regatta day and I made my way down to the start in an old rowing boat fitted with an outboard motor. The yachts were resplendent as they manoeuvred their highly coloured sails towards the starting line. Then, just as the cannon shot was about to begin the race, there descended a dramatic calm. The sails emptied, the ripples on the surface came to rest and Lough Erne reflected the boats and the blue summer sky in mirrored stillness. There wasn't a breath.

It would have been the perfect setting for a prayer of Dom Helder Camara:

Holy breathing of God, I feel you stirring.
Warmed by this breath good things start to grow.
Even in strong wealthy lands fresh mobilizing calls
Evoke planetary piety,
Winning the hearts and hands of the caring.
Each in a chosen path,
each with a special gift
take their stand to create a world more fit for living,
More just and more humane.

There is a quality in human life that is wild, irrepressible and free. In the face of war, famine, mountain ranges, desert wastes or terminal illness, there is this buoyant quality which we simply call human spirit. It invites us to dance when our feet are heavy, it wants us to sing when our voices are choked with grief, it wants us to smile in the face of pain. It plants a flower in the blitzed wilderness of war. We find in the feast of Pentecost the God Spirit which too defies description. Writers fall back on a variety of words like fire, dove, wind, or breath and each of them hints at ferment and unpredictability. Still, when we think of the Spirit of God as fire or wind we would prefer it to be contained. Comfortable arm-chair Christians would be happy with the Spirit as fire so long as it was the gentle log fire crackling in a winter fireplace. The Spirit as wind would be acceptable if it were the balmy breeze on a summer beach. 'Come Holy Spirit' is a dangerous prayer if we are not prepared for the consequences. We would have to get ready for the rush of God which would upset the siesta of our middle years by tearing through the sheltering places of our tidy lives and scattering all our careful plans and our well-filed prudence. St Paul, who was familiar with the prompting of the Spirit, tells us simply that:

> God's gift was not a Spirit of timidity,
> but the Spirit of power, and love and self-control.
> (2 Tim 1:7)

The Spirit may become an uncomfortable and embarrassing companion, for we could be led to reckless generosity in the face of world hunger; we may be propelled towards forgiveness when revenge would seem the quicker solution, and we may even be drawn to Christian unity when we would prefer the security of our own pews. Bishop Ignatius of Latikion, quoted at a recent Council of Churches at Upsala, put this all strikingly:

> Without the Holy Spirit
> God is far away
> Christ stays in the past
> The gospel is a dead letter
> The Church is simply an organisation.
>
> Authority is a matter of domination
> Mission is a matter of propaganda
> The liturgy no more than an evocation
> Christian living a slave mentality.

The summer day on Lough Erne never felt a breath of wind. The yachts with limp sails never moved from the starting stretch of water, and they stay in my mind as symbols of the well ordered, respectable, church-going Christian who is afraid to offer a hand to God in case the Spirit drags him into action. Father Cothrai Gogan, whose poetry I have admired for years, has the perfect Pentecost prayer:

> Come Spirit rain,
> precipitate, let fall and penetrate.
> Souse! Douse!
> Drench this dried up dust,
> and irrigate with coursing,
> living streams
> and showers this drought-struck me.
> Reach down.
> Bedew this dried-up deep-down self.
> Let sap revive.
> Let new life rise.
> Let greenwood greening meet all eyes,
> Now summer's come …

The kingdom within

It was one of those typical days in early January – one of those days when heavy showers of icy rain are swept down city streets by gusts of bitter wind. Those who had a pound or two left after the Christmas spending fever were out in search of bargains at the New Year sales, and they dodged the showers as they moved in relays from one store to the next. We were all caught by the suddenness of a midday downpour and I crushed my way into the front of a big department store and waited. The man beside me was protected by a large sandwich board and, with all the elbow room he could muster, he ate a well-washed apple with obvious signs of satisfaction.

I still vividly remember the scene as I stood there watching part of the life of a great city. Two women, grey faced, strained and tired were taking four eager children in search of anoraks when their own hearts must have been set on something new for themselves. There was an old man holding a newspaper over his wife's head to protect her from the icy shower while his own hair dripped beneath his collar. On the far side of the street, two lads in faded denims, who would be obvious candidates for a search later on, noticed an old man searching the litter basket at the bus stop, went back to offer him a few cigarettes and then stopped in the rain to give him a light. A mother behind me asked the security man at the store to search her handicapped son so that he wouldn't be made feel any different. Suddenly the rain ceased, and we eased our way on to the street. The sun had come out as the man with the sandwich board moved off. His message was direct and striking. The board read simply:

'The Kingdom of God is already amongst you.'

I never really understood that phrase from the Bible until then. The newspapers next morning would make headlines of the atrocities, but what the board said was that no camera could ever capture the elusive minute of God's presence. God, the poet tells us, is the bits and pieces of every day, but every day in the city for so long had been nothing but a catalogue of waste and worry and we, if we ever searched for God at all, would scarcely expect to find him there. Jesus Christ took on flesh and blood and made his home among mankind, and yet for centuries we have felt uncomfortable in his presence for we have stripped away flesh, drained him of his blood and tried to confine him to the inaccessible heights of a blue remote heaven.

This is what I imagine Christ was talking about when he said:
Open your eyes to the signs of the times.

Because he does slip into our lives in the guise of the poor who do exist even in the welfare state, in those imprisoned behind bars, or in the confines of a pensioner's bungalow. He is there among the least of his brothers and sisters, the least important, the least cared for. Christ is out and about and he will not be confined behind stained glass windows.

The rain came on again. People weighed down with plastic bags full of bargains filled the city cafes for lunch. I saw the sandwich board tucked tidily away beside a paper stall. The man had to eat too, I thought, or maybe he felt it was no weather for the word of God.

Sticks Maguire

It wasn't until his death notice appeared in the columns of the local paper that I got to know his Christian name. He had come to live in the bungalow at the foot of the village street years before, a frail remnant of what must have been, one day, a powerful man. We all knew him simply as 'Sticks Maguire', for he got around only with the help of two home-made crutches.

Some said he lost his leg in the great war, others had it that it was an accident in building one of those American railroads, but when one of us, coming home from school, plucked up enough courage to ask him one day, he told us a fascinating story about man-eating sharks in Australia.

He didn't go to church on Sundays, a bizarre bit of behaviour in a small village, which was all put down to gas in the trenches, things seen on the field of battle, or that word in the country which covers it all – oddness.

Now, when I come to think of it, we never blamed it on ourselves. Sticks attended every wake in the parish, more, I'll grant you, for the crack than commiserating with the bereaved, but he never was invited to many weddings or parish socials. He limped to the home games of the local football team and would wave one crutch in support or point it menacingly at the referee if the game was running against us. But he had to be content to sit on the bridge on Sunday evenings and wait for the first car home to hear how the team did on away match days, because no one thought of giving him a lift.

They say he went once to a week's mission in the parish but never went back. He wasn't a bitter man but he must have been amused and saddened by a neighbourhood which could work up an instant sympathy for the blind man at Jericho, the woman taken in adultery or the crippled man at the pool in Jerusalem, and all the time be blind themselves to the crippled man at the foot of their own town.

There was that continuing curiosity about the man during the years he lived with us. Where did he come from? Who were his people? What was he worth? But there was little interest in how he was coping with life in the years it was ebbing away from him.

For years I excused myself from the guilt of those days because I was at school then, but the village behaviour of those days has been repeated so often since. I find myself, now and again, moved to help the far off refugee, the starving family in Africa, the unknown deaf, the anonymous blind, while all around me I don't catch the urgency of the uncared for, or see the pain and loneliness of neighbours who carry quiet crosses with their shopping bags, or live with an agony that only shows itself in unguarded moments of weariness and fatigue.

And will we run breathless to God at the end of life, confident that we would have stood by his Son had we lived in Nazareth instead of Newtownards, or in Jerusalem instead of Belfast or Derry. Lord, when did we see you a stranger? – I hope he has the courtesy not to laugh.

We buried Sticks on a cold wet January day, unsure to the end of his denomination. An old woman at the grave expressed some surprise when they buried the crutches with him. In a way it was a fitting gesture. A Christian community had finally come to realise that those two sticks were the main support he had in the years he lived among us.

Harmony

Long before the days when orchestras advertised for transport managers, Dominic the fiddler, as he was known locally, could be seen most evenings making his way to wakes or weddings, céilís or crossroad gatherings, with his fiddle securely strapped, in its black box, to the carrier of his bicycle. It was no Stradivarius and he was no Yehudi Menhuin but if the music was wanted to distract grief, send someone off to America with a lighter heart, or to add to the joviality of the occasional wedding, then Dominic was your man.

His big hands, calloused with hard work, hadn't the delicate touch for the sensitive pieces but when he became conscious of the inadequacy of his performance, he drowned out the offending notes with great yelps, a recurring cough, or belted out the rhythm with his clognail boot on the wooden or stone floor.

The night his wife died, he hung the fiddle to a nail above the door and never played it again.

If you had asked Dominic why, he couldn't have given you any adequate reason but somehow he knew it was the right thing for him to do. Theirs was a happy marriage, based on a deep love for each other, which had grown in depth as they passed the years of their life together. He had a small farm and she was a farmer's daughter and they watched their children grow up with all the limitations of near poverty at times, and the dreaded possibility of emigration when the children were old enough to leave school. They took life's hurdles and setbacks together, one supporting the other with that strong undemonstrative love that expressed itself in

silent presence at the fireside, and in an unshakeable faith in the goodness of God. A daughter died with tuberculosis and, as they nursed her in a whitewashed outhouse, they found their mutual heartbreak was bringing them closer and closer together. Another son died on a battlefield in Europe and, as the others grew up and left home to start families of their own, they found themselves, one night, back where it all started – just two people sitting looking into the fire in an empty house.

The old fiddle was the story of their lives together. The music and harmony of life was produced by the two of them. Sometimes it was the lilting fiddle in the days of joy when the harvest was good and the children content. Sometimes it was the slow sad notes as death crossed the doorstep or sickness lingered. There were the days of the jarring notes too, when tempers got frayed and nerves set on edge because in-laws gave advice or the fair day lasted too long at the central bar.

When people at a function would applaud Dominic for his marathon music sessions, he would set aside any praise saying it was all a gift from God. It was the same God who gifted the pain and the promise, the better and the worse, the richness and the poverty of their days together, because without his blessing, they felt, the harmony might get out of tune or die out completely, and so it was until death snapped the strings.

Dominic's daughter lives with her family in the south of England. The old fiddle, beautifully polished now, hangs over the piano which she has bought for her little girl. 'She should be good at the piano,' she told me once, 'her grandfather was so musical.' I wasn't sure if I agreed but there was one thing certain. If she were a granddaughter of Dominic the fiddler and his wife, she would know the value of God-given life and be able to hear now and again the hidden harmony of the universe.

Parting

I heard them tell
around the glowing winter fires
that men and women
from around that same hearth
did take the stony mountain road
across the Sperrin gap
and somewhere above the shoulder of Dart mountain
they stood in choking grief
and snapped the valley
in their mind's eye
to have it with them
into blurred days
of Philadelphia and beyond.
This valley was my home until yesterday
I left the car in the autumn dawn
on the same gap
and called a blessing on its people
and the land from which they coaxed a living.
And, deep inside, I felt the grief
of ninety years ago
and knew again
their parting pain.

Nazareth Mansions 1961

Mary,
the news of your pregnancy
came as a complete surprise
wrapped up in the splendour
of the great angel's
whispered words.

My annunciation
happened in this joyless city flat
at nine fifteen
this morning.
An earthy brown unmarked envelope
held the clinic's accusing note.
The pregnancy test was positive
and I didn't hear
the rush of angel's wings.

Seven Last Words

It is finished

On this hillside I stand
beside your death bed
as I stood and watched helplessly
as my only son coughed up his thinning blood.
No crude nails riveted his hands
but his thin white arms were pocked with needle marks
which betrayed hours of narcotic numbness
when he was no longer mine.
He rose three times to see if therapy
could ease his thirst for cocaine
(In innocent days it numbed the gum before a tooth was pulled)
but every time the siren in his blood
cried out again for more.
And soon the captain of the team
could never get his place
and aged before my eyes
as friends turned away from him when all their efforts died.
Crucifixion killed you in a few short hours
so it mattered little that the nails were clean.
His vein sucked in death with a shot of heroin
and weakness swamped him for four long months
before his body, tired from resistance,
stole away in untimely death.
Now he is at peace for the craving disappeared
with his dying breath.

I thirst

With tired arms and arthritic fingers
I lift you up this cup of cold water.
I too have known the burning thirst.
Years before the wealth of womanhood had dawned on me
in solemn vow I gave myself to you the risen Christ
gone beyond flesh and the dizzy rush of blood.
In cold convent chapels I craved your closeness
and put up with pointless pettiness,
with rules which robbed me of spontaneity
hoping that at the end of the meandering maze
I might find you.
But the years of thin theology
and bustling busyness and being hard on the body
left me drained of loving
when I came to the celebration of a silver jubilee.
Now the sun shines through the stained glass window
as I sit in the convent chapel for the last time.
Tomorrow we all move out.
In a few months a supermarket will stand here
offering bread and wine for a price.
But I kept my vow and stayed. I'm happy to know that you, the
Christ, know thirst.
For you will slake my thirst with living water
even thought it's getting late.

Why have you forksaken me?

There was a day of unbridled joy
a day when colour, love and faith ran riot.
We had given each to other for life
in days of lilting joy or stumbling darkness before your altar.
My three boys, all born without a blemish,
were the crowning grace.
Then, one day, he was gone with another woman
without a word of explanation or apology
I kept bitterness at bay for the sake of the children
but when they go to bed I pick my steps through the valley of
darkness
and even you, forsaken Christ, seem seldom at my side
Rejection is suffering without honour.
People are polite, at least to my face,
but the children cannot boast about their father
my husband, my lover
the man who walked away with all my secrets.
I used to pray myself to sleep
counting grief on beads
but I stand now,
forsaken like you,
waiting your touch to give sense to my suffering
and purpose to my pain.

Father forgive them,
for they know not what they do

I always thought that Golgotha was near Jerusalem
until the week before Christmas
when the policeman, with the marked Antrim accent
spoke about a shooting.
The Christmas tree held no greenery that year
for it was a stark cross of wood.
My son grew up tense and troubled
with evening news bulletins about death in his native city
He left it for a while to see if exile would heal his heartache
but Belfast called him home with its unequalled friendship
and the humour of the streets.
His wife and sons were the centre of his life
and he gave hours to building community
so that the boys might inherit peace
in this city where human blood
slick-like polluted the sidewalks.
But they killed the gentle man because he had a vision
and could see beyond the walls that herded people
and fed them on dividing myths
Two thieves on a motorbike stole his life
and Calvary was closer than I ever thought
and words of forgiveness are stilled
within my confused and troubled mind.
'Father, forgive them' still carries no conviction.

Today you will be with me
in paradise

The closest I came to Paradise
was the May morning I stood beside the man I loved
in full bridal splendour.
The promises were so easy – to love and cherish all the days of a
future together
But spring gave way to winter after the briefest of summers
I thought the fault was mine.
Was it my sunny nature, my love of life
which stirred the jealousy that led to that first numbing blow?
The precarious days of pregnancy saw no respite.
Later the baby would cry out his protest at
the violent world but the string of accusations
rolled down the years, with all their back up bouts of frenzied
violence
The first black eye I blamed on the baby's head
but the excuses ran out when I couldn't show up
at my child's first communion
because of the drunken insanity of the night before
when the boy, fear filled, hid all night with his dog
and him dressed up in the suit I borrowed from my sister.
For the sake of the children, I took the tongue lashing
and the physical assaults in sullen defiant silence.
The veiled threat of a domestic massacre kept us together
until I found the courage to lift my children
and steal way when whiskey sank him to a drugged sleep
and dulled his senses.
The home for battered wives has limited luxuries.
There is the endless uncertainty about the years ahead.

But thanks, Jesus, for being close to me on Calvary
for this place to me is the closest I felt to paradise
since the May morning of my marriage eight long years ago.

Father, into your hands
I commend my spirit

Gone in her sixteenth year.
She faced the wild Atlantic
stepping into its hungry waves alone.
Hooked on despair, she concluded youth to be an end
and not the beginning of life's adventure.
I heard her first deep breath
beyond the pain of birth
but wasn't with her when the stormy winter ocean
stilled the life in her.
And she was so particular about her hair
and always wore a bathing cap
and hated the swimming pool when
the school had its hour on Mondays
Where did we fail her? Why didn't we see
the shadows that fell over her?
But then I catch glimpses and find her full of joy
like the summer days
when she splashed laughter into her sister's face
on the shore of Ballybunion
My life is drained of joy as I watch her father
sink into grief with each day's ending
wondering if he had ever said to her that his love for her
was his deepest inner joy
Her life, like an old film, has been run before our eyes
over and over again
but I cannot see that point of pain
that beckoned her to the hungry sea.
Father, into your hands, I commend her wild free spirit
and also take my own – now broken.

Woman behold your son

I always thought you were a bit abrupt at Cana
when you called your mother 'woman'.
But wasn't it a hint about this day
when your hour has come at last?
But God, weren't you a bit abrupt with me
in that hospital ward when I couldn't give a second glance
at my new born baby
because of the foreign features which marked his handicap.
I didn't speak to you for six soured years
because of your divine clumsiness.
A teacher, years ago, pointed to your handiwork
on the patterns of frost across the winter window panes
or in the first delicate petals of spring.
'God is the master craftsman' she would say,
her voice trailing away in admiration.
But where, I wondered were you, when my child
was being fashioned in the womb
was the only thought which filled my mind.
Then on a Good Friday I heard Isaiah describe you as having
'no looks to attract our eyes
without beauty, without majesty'.
And once again I looked hard at my child
and discovered he was the living image of yourself
'Woman behold your son.'
And so I did and have stood beside him ever since
and have come to know him as another gentle prophet
in a world of comfortless sounds.